THE PENN
OF
DENN

The world through Denn coloured glasses.

Graham
Thanks for your ministry
@ Cornerstone this Morning -
Hope you enjoy the Penn

Denn Guptill

forever books
WINNIPEG, CANADA
www.foreverbooks.ca

Cover Design: Jason Vienneau
Book Design: Andrew Mackay
Managing Editor: Beryl Henne

Forever Books

WINNIPEG CANADA
www.foreverbooks.ca

Contents

Introduction

The Penn of Denn had its beginning late in the last century on a whim. I was doing up the bulletin for the official opening of Bedford Community Church and thought I should write a greeting of some kind. I realized I would need some type of title for the blurb.

I worked through the usual suspects: "From the pastor's desk," as if anything could be found on my desk. "The pastor's pen" sounded promising, except I was using a computer.

Somewhere along the line, I realized that my name went very well with Pen except for the spelling. Never one to let a little thing like the English language stand in my way, "Penn of Denn" seemed fine for what it was, a one-off greeting. The next week I heard something and thought it would be a great "Penn." The next week it was something I read.

Over the past 700 weeks there have been times I have struggled with what to write, but for the most part I heard, saw, or read something that proclaimed "This would be a great Penn of Denn." I don't think I have ever written as the result of someone saying "You should write about …" My response is usually "That's why it called the Penn of Denn and not the Penn of _____."

I'm not trying to be rude—well not really rude—it's just that the Penn has become a part of who I am and how I view things.

In 2001, when Bedford Community Church was going through one of its valleys and I knew I would have to look at working outside the church again, an editor I knew offered me a freelance writing gig for three magazines she edited based solely on having read the Penn of Denn. Over the next four years, I would have the opportunity to write for a half a dozen different magazines on topics as diverse as tall ships and natural gas pipelines.

I appreciated the work and the pay, but it was work— except for a column I produced for Atlantic Boating News called "Aboat Time." Like the Penn, it allowed me to be me. I've included a few "Aboat Times" as my closing chapter.

While I consider myself to be not a bad writer, my grammar is atrocious, so I would be remiss if I didn't thank by beautiful wife, Angela, and all my other proofreaders through the years for making me look smarter than I really am. Stan Wickwire, Bonnie Barteaux, Greg Hanson, and Michele Meade have done a great job.

Thank you to Judy Savoy, a really funny lady who takes

grammar and punctuation seriously, for doing my final proof-read. www.judysavoy.com

So, enjoy meandering through my take on life, the church, and the world around me.

And be warned the journey won't always take you down the politically correct path.

It's All About the Church

IT IS GREAT TO have each one of you out this morning. As most of you know, this service is the beginning of a new chapter in the life of BBC (Bedford Community Church). We would like to invite you to be part of that adventure with us.

If you are visiting from another church, we thank you for coming. Our prayer is that God will bless you as you work in your local church. However, if you don't have a regular church home, we'd love to have you join us for worship each week at this time.

If you would like to see me or have coffee together, please indicate on the communication card. If your need is urgent, please indicate it by circling *A* on the card. Thanks again for coming—I trust that we will see you again.

DID YOU HAVE ENOUGH spiders this fall? Incredible, the number of arachnids we had around the outside of our house last month. Mind you, having lived in Australia for four years—where you could saddle the spiders and ride them like ponies—it wasn't a particular threat.

It wasn't the spiders I minded; live and let live, right? It was the webs. There is nothing more annoying and frightening than walking into a web, unless it's the thought you had down under: what spun the web could weigh as much as a small puppy. Yuck!

Spiders aren't the only things that have webs. So do we! Webs of influence and webs of relationships that are all interconnected to the centre—you. I was told recently that, on average, churched believers have a relationship of some kind with seven people who aren't in church or in Christ. It might be a co-worker or someone you share a hobby with. It might be the parents of your kids' friends or a relative. Who is in your web? Maybe it's time you actually took the time to see whom you could introduce to your church and whom you could introduce to your Lord. After all, it might make an eternity of difference.

I SAT IN AN old, cold, and draughty church last week listening to a scratchy sound system, sitting on a hard pew for forty minutes longer then they told me I would have to. It suddenly dawned on me why so many people don't go to church anymore.

I wondered to myself, "Self, how many people does this represent church to? How many people have this as a memory of the house of God?" The paint was peeling, there was hardly any parking, and I realized that it had the air of a once-prosperous business that had failed to compete and now had no future. But why? Is the product now inferior to the competition or was it all in presentation? Does God belong to yesterday? Is He only a God of old buildings and century-old music? Or does He actually have something to say to those who live in the era of computer chips and shopping malls?

If God is seen as out-of-date and irrelevant, is that God's fault or the fault of those who portray Him as the God of yesterday? Let's remember that we worship the God of yesterday, today, and tomorrow!

I WAS IN THE hospital this week! It wasn't anything serious. As a matter of fact, it wasn't anything at all. You see, I wasn't admitted. I was just visiting, which is really fortunate because hospitals make me very uncomfortable.

I don't know what it is. Maybe it's just my preconceptions … the beds look hard, the company looks depressing and so does the food, not to mention the lovely shade of green they chose for their walls. Maybe I'm wrong though. Maybe the beds really are comfortable, the company stimulating, and the food delicious, after all I've been wrong before. Twice.

In spite of all my preconceptions, I think that hospitals are great places to be if you're sick or broken. Jesus said in Luke 5:31-32, *"Jesus answered them, 'Healthy people don't need a doctor—sick people do. I have come to call not those who think they are righteous, but those who know they are sinners and need to repent.'"* Let's try to remember that BCC wasn't planted just for the righteous but also to call sinners to repentance.

It's All About the Church

ARE YOU HERE WITH a friend today? Did you bring a friend today? I hope so. The reality of the situation is that most Christians came to know Jesus Christ through the influence of friends or relatives. Pastors influenced 6 percent of believers, Sunday School had an impact on 4 percent, while Evangelistic Crusades and T.V. programs are responsible for a whopping .001 percent of all conversions. 80 percent of Christians credit friends or family with leading them into their relationship with Jesus Christ and His church.

It was only through the perseverance of Reg Thomas that I came to know Christ. If Reg had of stopped inviting me to church and sharing Jesus with me when I told him to stop, where would I be today? Chances are I wouldn't be here. But Reg's concern for my salvation wouldn't let him stop. Thank you, Reg.

Perhaps your friend didn't come today. That's OK. Maybe they really did have to wash their hair or wax their car. One of my friends had to go to Newfoundland, but I'm going to invite her again. Thanks for taking the time to invite a friend. Even if they didn't come this time, maybe they will next time.

THE HEADLINES SAY IT all: "Bikers Hold Party In Former Church." It seems that Winnipeg's Los Brovos bike gang hosted a party at their club house—the former Filipino United Community Church.

The article went on to talk about how what used to be the altar is now a stand-up bar, complete with sliding glass coolers and freezers. "There's a confessional in there and everything," said one member of Satan's Choice, laughing. "We confessed our sins."

While disturbing at first, the reality is that the party was simply held in a building—not a church, not even a former church—just a building where a church used to meet. After all, what makes a building a church? The answer, of course, is the things that happen in it. When God's people get together to praise and worship their Lord they are the church. That happens if they worship in a grand cathedral complete with stain glass and a pipe organ, or if they worship in a little country chapel complete with wood stove and pump organs, or even if they worship in a movie theatre complete with a giant screen and surround sound.

It's All About the Church

I WAS OUT SHOPPING the other night and everything was a blur. It wasn't because we are getting closer to the Christmas season and everything is busy and the stores are jammed with people. It wasn't because I was in a hurry and had to rush. It was because I'd forgotten my glasses at home.

Because I wear my glasses all the time ... well, most of the time ... well, the times I don't leave them at home, I forget how fuzzy things can be without them. It's kind of like the clarity we have when we look at things through Christ's eyes. He allows us to see things the way they should be instead of the way they are. When you look around and see friends and family who don't know Jesus personally, are you tempted to think "It'll never happen?" Or do you see them where they could be, in a growing dynamic relationship with Christ? When you see BCC do you see it the way it is or do you see it the way it will be? Because you'll never know how fuzzy things are until you see how clear they can be. And you'll never see things clearly until you look through *His* eyes.

I SAT IN A meeting today that lasted forever, at least it seemed like it lasted forever. I was reminded that you never get a second chance to make a first impression. They introduced a man who was there primarily to sell me a product ... a product that I was at least a little interested in—after all, I went to their presentation. By all accounts it was a good product, but after he had wasted an hour of my time with repetitive, condescending remarks, he would have had to give the product to me for me to take it.

It is so true that a product is known by its representatives. It brought home to me my responsibility as a representative of Christ and His Kingdom. The question for each one of us as a believer is "How do we impact people's view of Jesus?" Will people be attracted to the Gospel through our lives or will we have turned them off to Christ's claims because of our behaviour or our speech? My prayer is that my behaviour and who I am will never cause a person to reject Christ for who He is. I hope that is your prayer as well.

It's All About the Church

I WAS STUNNED. WELL, some things go without saying, but this time I had a reason. Last Sunday when I arrived at the Lion's Den to set up for worship I discovered that the locks on both of our storage boxes had been broken off and the tops had been removed. Our church had been broken into, and we don't even have a church building. When I pastored in Truro it had almost gotten to be old hat to have the church broken into but I thought those days were behind me. On Monday I discovered that the Lion's Den had been broken into the week before and the bar had been robbed. (Guess that's one of the downsides of having a bar in church.) On the bright side nothing was taken from our boxes or damaged. To paraphrase Matthew Henry's response after he had been robbed by highwaymen, I'm thankful that although the locks were broken there wasn't more damage, and I'm thankful that although the boxes were opened nothing was stolen. But most of all I'm thankful that I was the one who was broken into and that I wasn't the one who did the breaking in.

I DIDN'T UNDERSTAND A word he said. I was in Ottawa a couple of weeks ago and I had the opportunity to visit the Parliament buildings. After the tour our group decided to watch question period from the visitor's gallery, you know … to watch our government in action. On the way from the Peace Tower to the Gallery I passed a security guard who was under the mistaken impression that I spoke French. Boy was he wrong! I presume he was trying to be helpful because he gestured down the hall toward the open doors of the visitor's gallery and gave me directions in French. Being a little too proud, I merely nodded and continued on my way. I sure hope he was giving me directions.

As I walked down the hall I lamented that I couldn't speak both our official languages. Then I wondered if we confused guests in our church when we speak "Christianeze." I don't mean watering down the essentials but are churches the only buildings with foyers instead of lobbies? Can't we pray that someone will have a safe trip instead of asking for travelling mercies? It just takes a minute to translate our church language back into English for our guests.

It's All About the Church

I WAS TALKING TO a gentleman the other day who had recently moved to Halifax from British Columbia. He told me he was really enjoying living in the Maritimes but wondered how long it would be until he was no longer considered a "CFA." I must have looked confused because he explained that people would often comment, "Oh you 'come from away.'" Talk about making people feel at home. I realized that we can be friendly without ever letting people feel like they belong.

I wonder how often people come away from church feeling like a "CFA?" They leave feeling like they weren't a part of the group and might never be. If we are doing our job as a church then we should be reaching those who come from away, those who have been away from God and now are on their journey home. Part of our job is to make them feel at home and to help make their return a little bit easier. We need to treat our guests as if they belong and welcome them as a part of the family, not like they are strangers who stumbled into a private party.

IT WAS KIND OF neat. This week I received a letter and a tape from a pastor in Georgia. He explained that he had downloaded one of my sermons from sermoncentral.com, modified it, and preached it in his church. He thanked me for the message and sent along the tape of his sermon as a thank-you. As I listened to his tape I realized that close to half his message was my words—I mean literally! My words. I pulled my manuscript up on the computer and followed along as he preached my message, complete with my stories and jokes ... everything but my lisp. A little eerie, but very flattering. I e-mailed Sam, thanking him for treating my message with respect in the way that he preached it. He really did a great job. But as I listened to the tape I wondered how I would have felt if Sam had butchered my message and carelessly used my words without realizing or caring about the work that went into them. That made me realize how God must feel when we misuse His words, His message. It's not just words, it's God's *Word,* so let's make sure we treat it with the love and respect it deserves.

It's All About the Church

I Was Reading …

LAST WEEK I WAS reading my latest Men's Health magazine. Five pages into it a two-page ad caught my attention. It said, "Do not look for answers to the wrong questions. Will you eventually be asked how big your office was or how much money you made? But tell your inquisitors you swam under a waterfall and climbed a 200-foot cedar. Tell them how to run a class five rapid. Tell them the answer is El Capitan, then ask them what the question is. Be selfish about this. Let that body of yours feel its way up a rock face and find its balance on the slippery slope in a creek. When you reach the top or get to the other side, look back. See what you've put behind you. Now, only one question deserves an immediate answer. What else is there?"

This was an ad for "Nike." But life isn't about sneakers, it's about life. The criteria for a full life isn't shooting rapids or wearing "Nikes," it's your relationship with others and with God.

I READ AN ARTICLE this past week that said we will spend five years of our life waiting in line! There have been times I've felt like I waited five years in one line. That doesn't even begin to include the time we spend waiting on the phone, waiting at red lights and stop signs, and waiting in doctor's and dentist's offices. If you are like me, you probably don't like waiting; nothing seems to irritate me more than waiting for something to happen. In the case of the dentist's office, it almost seems perverse to be waiting for what's going to happen there! But sometimes, in this super-fast world, waiting is the only time we get to think. The Old Testament prophet Isaiah wrote *"But those who trust in the LORD will find new strength. They will soar high on wings like eagles. They will run and not grow weary. They will walk and not faint"* (Isa 40:31).

This week, why not take a little bit of time to wait on the Lord, a little bit of time to ask Him, "God, what are your plans for my life?" He might have a pleasant surprise in store for you.

THE COVER STORY OF this week's Time Magazine is about "Redux." Ever hear of it? No? It's the first diet pill approved in the US in twenty-three years and it is sweeping the United States. Coming soon, I'm sure, to a pharmacy near you. This new wonder drug has been on the market for only five months, but doctors are already writing 85,000 prescriptions a week. Why not? "Redux" tricks the body into believing it's full, thereby reducing our desire for food. The company projects sales in excess of one billion dollars (that's nine zeros) in five years.

Not bad for a drug that can cause fatigue, diarrhea, vivid dreams, dry mouth, has caused permanent brain damage in animals, and can trigger a rare but often fatal human disorder that destroys blood vessels in the lungs and heart. But then again … I guess it beats self-control.

I understand, though, you can do the same without the side effects if you just focus on fruit … the fruit of the Spirit that is.

I READ THE OTHER day that the most frequently asked question today is ... "Would you like fries with your order?" Profound to say the least. Now, I did not read that the most important question asked today was "Would you like fries with your order?" It's just the most frequently asked, although I'm sure that to some it is a very important question. The reason the question is asked so frequently is that it is in reality an example of "suggestive sales." Just by asking the question, they are increasing the chances of you buying fries with your meal, as if your meal wouldn't be complete without fries.

The most important question that can be asked today is the same question that held that honour 2,000 years ago ... and it was asked over and over again, "What must I do to inherit eternal life?" The answer is the same now as it was when Jesus answered it then, in John 3:3, *"I tell you the truth, unless you are born again, you cannot see the Kingdom of God."*

The answer to the other question is "No, if I'd wanted fries, I would have asked for them."

I Was Reading ...

I READ AN ARTICLE the other day in which the author wrote of maintaining a list of the fifty things she wanted to try before she died. When the writer accomplished one of her goals, she would scratch it off and add something new to the bottom of the list.

What would you put on a list like that? What are some of the things that you would like to do before you die? Learn to ride a horse? Fly a plane? Jump out of a plane? Write a book? Read a book? Scuba dive?

I would presume that the list would be different for every one of us because we all have different dreams and different desires. The common denominator with each one of us, though, should be the desire to stretch and grow, the desire to not just live but live life to the fullest. You may not be able to determine how many years you will get in your life, but it will be your choice as to how much life you get in your years.

When you make your list, could I make a suggestion? Sure I can, after all, it's my column. Consider putting down, "Lead someone to Christ." It'll be the only thing on the list that you can take with you.

I FOUND OUT THE other day I only have 500 days to live. That's only a year and a half. It was quite a shock when I found out. It wasn't my doctor who told me, it was something I read, an article by Leslie Flynn entitled "If You Are 35, You have 500 days to live." Its thesis was that when you subtract the time sleeping, working, tending to personal matters, hygiene, odd chores, medical matters, eating, travelling, and miscellaneous time stealers, in the next thirty-six years you will have roughly the equivalent of only five hundred days left to spend as you wish. Now that is certainly food for thought. 500 days, wow. Many of you have less than that. So, the question begs to be asked, "What are you going to do with your 500 days?" After all, it really is up to you. Nobody else can spend that time for you. You may allow them to steal it from you but it will be your decision. Is it any wonder that Jesus' brother James wrote in James 4:14, *"How do you know what your life will be like tomorrow? Your life is like the morning fog—it's here a little while, then it's gone."*

The choice is yours. Are you just going to put in time and try to get the most years in your life, or are you going to try to get the most life in your years? 500 days, Wow! Think about it. You have 500 days with which to do exactly as you please.

Just Stuff

REBECCA WAS TELLING US last week that when her brother was little, he thought colour was a recent innovation. He thought in the old days everything was black and white! It may seem silly, but wasn't that a reasonable assumption? All of the pictures that Adam had seen of that time were black and white, and the old movies and old television programs were in black and white.

There are people who go through life never seeing the colours. They might as well be living in a world painted in various shades of grey. Their life is one of drudgery not of beauty. But that isn't what God wants for us! God has given us a palette of colours, and it's up to us as to how we are going to paint our lives. The difference between ordinary and extraordinary is the little extra.

I SAW A SIGN in a doctor's office once that had a profound effect on how I view life and how I approach it in most cases. The sign said, "Don't take life too seriously, because you'll never get out of it alive!" Deep? Profound? Have you stopped and smelled the roses today? Have you slowed down a little bit from the rush to just enjoy life? Too busy? Too much to do? You'd better do your best to enjoy life 'cause you aren't going to get out of it alive.

"You don't understand how busy I am, Denn!" No, I probably don't, but I do know we often allow the urgent to take precedence over the important. The question that begs to be asked is "What is important?" And you know as well as I do that what is important for me may not be important for you, and vice versa. But there are some things that are universally important, or at least should be, so we need to ask, are you spending enough time with your family? With your God? With yourself? For that last one, I don't mean working, I mean enjoying your own company, reflecting on who you are and how you can be better, as a person.

Why not take a little time today and find a rose to smell, a sunset to watch, or a pond to dip your feet in!

Last week I commented to Greg on how snow removal had suffered since amalgamation, to which he replied, "You blame everything on amalgamation." That isn't entirely true, although I am convinced that it has something to do with the weird weather we've been having lately! (Now that the cold war's over and we can't blame the Russians for everything, we need a substitute.)

It's easy to place the blame for things we don't like firmly at someone else's feet. Sometimes we do the very same thing in our spiritual life. Back in the '70's, comedian Flip Wilson used to remark "The devil made me do it." That may be out of vogue now, but how many times have you heard believers blame the "Demon of Anger" or the "Demon of Lust" or the "Demon of whatever?" I do believe that Satan is real and that Screwtape and his buddies are real, but sometimes I think we are just looking for a scapegoat to blame for our lack of spiritual discipline. Now, if I could only find a way to blame my lack of self-control on amalgamation!

I MADE AN EXCITING discovery the other day. You gotta love that when it happens, you know it's a serendipitous moment (look it up in the dictionary). It wasn't a lost continent or anything like that, but it was a happy discovery nevertheless.

I was listening to a CD that I've listened to countless times before and when the last track ended, instead of simply shutting down, it started counting backwards. I waited for almost two full minutes until another song started, one that wasn't mentioned on the disk itself or in the liner notes. Neat, Huh?

I thought to myself, how often are we like that with God? How often are we so anxious to get on with the next thing on our agenda that we miss out on what God might have in store for us?

The Bible tells us in Psalm 46:10 our God says, *"Calm down, and learn that I am God!"* Hard to do though, isn't it? Calm down, that is. But how many times have we rushed right past the gold that God wanted us to discover on our way to play in the dirt? Maybe we need to heed the words of the man who said "Don't just do something, stand there." Maybe we'll have a serendipitous moment courtesy of God.

Just Stuff

WELL, THE CALL FINALLY came. I'd been waiting for it for twenty years, but it was still a little bit of a surprise when it finally came.

Talk about a veritable roller coaster of emotions. I didn't know if I should be excited or depressed.

The call came late one evening from an old acquaintance, not even a real close friend. She said, very simply, "I'm calling about our twenty-year high school reunion." How old would I have to be to have graduated twenty years ago?

Now, on the one hand, I'm really excited about seeing old friends and finding out what people have done with their lives. On the other hand, I ask myself, how will I measure up in their eyes? Where am I, twenty years down the road? Have I fulfilled my dreams and aspirations? Maybe like the Apostle Paul I need to adopt Philippians 4:11 as my credo, *"I have learned how to be content with whatever I have."*

But don't be fooled, I am secure with who I am and what I've done with my life. And, if anyone should ask, I weigh 195 pounds, I pastor a church of 3,000 people, and I am vice president of marketing with Tip Top.

LET ME TELL YOU, I felt like a fool—a feeling that is not necessarily unfamiliar to me. I had adjusted the sign for the church and stepped back to admire my handiwork. In doing so I stepped into a hole, twisted my ankle, and fell into a pile. My first thought was "That hurt;" my second thought, which occurred almost simultaneously, was "I hope no one was watching." Isn't pride a wonderful thing?

I ignored the pain for most of the morning but by lunch I was ready to have someone look at it. The doctor at the Cobequid looked at my foot, had it X-rayed, and told me that I had a nasty sprain. He proceeded to have it taped and gave me a list of instructions to help expedite the healing process, a list that I looked at and promptly forgot. After all, what were the chances of me staying off my foot for forty-eight hours?

Well, here we are more than two weeks later, my foot is still bothering me, and people tell me it serves me right, because I didn't follow the doctors instructions. Can you imagine?

It's kind of like not following the instructions that God lays out in His Word, the Bible, and then blaming the consequences on the church or God. The doctor didn't tell me not to walk for two days so he could ruin my fun. He did it to heal my foot. The Bible wasn't given to ruin our fun, God gave us His word to heal our souls.

Just Stuff

Do you ever feel in over your head? This week is kind of like that for me. With work responsibilities (BCC & Tip Top), Bedford Days, Beulah camp, and trying to make a little bit of time for family, I feel like I'm just treading water. Actually, there are times that I feel like I'm not quite treading water.

And so I dug out a paper my mother recently gave me entitled "19 Creative Ways to Handle Stress." I have always felt when I find something useful that I need to share it with those around me. So, here are the cream of the crop:

1. Pop some popcorn without putting the lid on.
2. When someone says "Have a nice day," tell them you have other plans.
3. Make a list of things "to do" that you have already done.
4. Retaliate for tax woes by filling out your tax forms in roman numerals.
5. Pay your electric bills in pennies.
6. Drive to work in reverse.
7. Read the dictionary upside down and look for secret messages.
8. Start a rumour and see if you recognize it when it comes back to you.
9. Bill your doctor for the time spent in his waiting room.
10. Make up a language and ask people for directions.

Of course if those don't work you could always try Peter's advice in 1 Peter 5:7, *"Give all your worries and cares to God, for he cares about you."*

THE END IS NEAR, the end is near! Not necessarily the end of the world, just the end of June. You may recall that last week I spoke about being a little stressed. This week, that became a lot stressed, and I certainly do appreciate all of you who have been praying for me and my family. That's all a part of what the Bible means when it says in Galatians 6:2 you obey the law of Christ when you offer each other a helping hand.

After a number of people spoke to me about the stress busters that I included in the Penn of Denn last week I thought I would include the rest of the list this week, so here goes:

1. Use your MasterCard to pay off your Visa.
2. Forget the diet and send yourself a candygram.
3. Tape pictures of your boss or teacher on watermelons and launch them from high places.
4. Put your toddler's clothes on backwards and send him off to school as if nothing was wrong.
5. Leaf through a National Geographic and draw bathing suits on the natives.
6. Relax by mentally reflecting on your favourite episode of "The Flinstones" during that important meeting.
7. Stare at people through the tines of a fork and pretend they're in jail.

The end is near, and until it gets here I really appreciate your prayers. Thanks.

Just Stuff

GREG BOUGHT A BOOK over the holidays entitled *The 100 Most Important Events In Christian History*. In the course of conversation, he asked me what I would consider to fit into that category. It didn't take me very long to come to my conclusion. "My salvation," I replied. But what about the Reformation, the Crusades, Wesley's conversion, and Billy Graham's 1949 crusade in Los Angeles?

Oh sure, they were important—maybe even earth shattering—but in my opinion they pale in comparison to September 2, 1979, when I surrendered my life to Jesus Christ. I wasn't terrible, I hadn't robbed a liquor store or killed anyone, but I was in need of God and had done nothing to deserve His favour. He reached down from heaven, forgave the sins of a young fisherman, and made him a child of the King.

My conversion may not get me into Greg's book, but it did get me into God's book. That has to be one of the most important events in Christian history, at least the way I see it. Your salvation is every bit as important as mine, or Wesley's, or Augustine's.

HAVE YOU EVER SAID anything you later regretted? You know, made a statement about the future that seemed like a sure thing at the time only to have it come back and haunt you, over and over and over again. Maybe it was an "I'm gonna do this" or "I'll never do that" kind of statement, or maybe it was just a prediction about the way things were going to turn out. The worst part is that people never seem to remember the times we were right, they just keep harping on that one dumb statement that we made.

I'm not sure how many times I've read the statement made by Bill Gates "640 Kilobytes ought to be enough for anybody." (Although Gates claims he never made the statement, I wouldn't admit to it either.)

It seems that people forget what Gates has done, for better or worse, and all they can see is this one really dumb prediction. Aren't you glad that God doesn't keep track of the really dumb things we say or the really dumb things we do. When we turn away from our sins and turn to God, His word tells us that along with His forgiveness comes the promise of His forgetfulness.

YIKES, HAVE YOU FILLED your tank lately? It's obviously gone too far. Gas now cost as much as Barq's root beer. Of course, gas comes from a non-renewable resource and requires an incredible amount of technology and expense to go from crude oil to a consumer product and Barq's is just sugar, water and artificial flavouring, but let's leave that alone.

What has struck me as funny during this entire fuel crunch—remember that I drive a V8, so I need to find something funny about it—is how skewed our sense of expense is. Cheap milk is $1.41 a litre, cheap orange juice is over a buck a litre, and for those who drink the demon rum, well it'd be a whole lot cheaper if you drank gasoline. The point is that we use a whole lot more gas than milk, OJ, or even Barq's, so it costs more.

It's the same with our spiritual lives ... There are things that cost less than being a disciple of Jesus Christ, but those things are unable to give us the power we need for living, so we have to make a choice. The truth is this: if we want the power then we have to pay the price.

I PURCHASED A SOFT drink while I was on the road the other day and the label informed me that I had a one-in-four chance of winning. Winning what, I'm not sure. Being the cynic that I am, I automatically translated that into having a three in four chance of losing, which I did.

With that in mind, I still bought the soft drink, opened the soft drink, drank the soft drink, and even looked under the cap to confirm that I had lost. I may be a cynic but I'm a practical cynic. If by some cosmic misunderstanding I should have won, I would have claimed the prize, whatever the prize was.

There are people out there today, maybe even someone reading this, who won't accept the forgiveness that Jesus can offer because they are a little cynical. After all, it can't be that simple, can it? Because of their cynicism they will never experience that forgiveness, they will never experience the fullness of life that only Christ can give, they will never experience fellowship with God, and ultimately they will die and go to hell. All because they think it can't be that simple. But it is.

I COULDN'T BELIEVE MY eyes. The last time I had seen James Morrison he was in the praise band at a Wesleyan camp I was attending just outside of Sydney, Australia. Then I saw him last week, wearing a white dinner jacket, playing his trumpet for the whole world to hear. Maybe you saw him too. He led the band at the opening ceremonies for the 2000 Olympics. Even though playing for the Olympics must have been a high point in the career of one of Australia's greatest musicians, an even greater honour lies ahead for him, because someday James Morrison will play in the praise band that gathers around the throne of God.

Do you ever stop to think about heaven? Think about how great it will be to sing our praises to God. Do you ever yearn to be with the one you call Lord, or are you so comfortable here that heaven almost seems a step down? The day will come, honest, and if you're a believer it will be a homecoming like you can't even begin to imagine. Maybe you'll even get to sing on the worship team that James plays for.

IT WAS TWENTY YEARS ago this month. Twenty years. It doesn't seem that long, but I guess it's been half a lifetime for me. It was January 1981, and I was a second year student at Bethany Bible College when I became the pastor of a little church in Saint John, NB. They were without a pastor and, at twenty dollars a service for a twenty-year-old Bible College student who had only preached three sermons, it seemed like a pretty good deal. Recently I looked at some of the messages I preached while I was there and felt like I should refund their money.

Being a preacher really wasn't the plan; at least it wasn't my plan. I was supposed to be a pilot flying missionaries into the remote areas of the world. But the preaching thing seems to have worked out all right. Twenty years, four churches, three countries, and two continents later … here I am. For twenty years I've done what I love and have loved what I've done, and that seems like a pretty good deal to me. So here's to another twenty years. Thanks to all of you for being a part of the adventure.

Just Stuff

THE MAIL ALWAYS GETS through, eventually. A post card arrived in Aberdeen, Scotland, last week from Brisbane, Australia. No major surprises there, but the card had been mailed on January 4th. 6 weeks isn't the speed of light, but it's pretty standard for surface mail from "Down Under." The problem is the card wasn't sent 6 weeks before. It was sent 5830 weeks before. That's right, the post card had been mailed on January 4th, 1889. That's a hundred and twelve years ago. Aberdeen postmaster Peter Smith said "We have no idea where it's been." Really?

Do you ever feel like your prayers have gone wherever Colin Wadrop's postcard had been stored? We need to remember that unanswered prayers aren't unheard prayers. The problem in my life was that unless God answered the way Denn thought He should, it was considered unanswered prayer. Gradually I'm learning that God is smarter than Denn and that not everything Denn asks for in prayer is always in Denn's best interest.

There is a remote chance that if God is smarter than Denn, He might be smarter than you. So maybe your prayers have been answered, just not in the way you expected.

IT WAS SUPPOSED TO be a great religious awakening, a return to our spiritual heritage. In the weeks immediately following the tragedy of September 11th, churches, synagogues, and mosques across North America saw an increase in their regular worship attendance.

Leaders of all faiths spoke about the impact the terrorist attacks had on people's lives and how it had drawn people closer to God.

The rubble has yet to be cleared from ground zero, and already it would appear the surge in church attendance was only a temporary spike. If there was an awakening it didn't last very long, and our countries have returned to their spiritual naps. Once again we are seemingly oblivious to the God we called out to ten weeks ago. But that shouldn't be surprising in the life of a nation because that's often the way it goes in our own lives. We are quick to call out to God when things are tough, we get laid off, our spouse gets sick, or the kids rebel. But what about when things are all right? Our Heavenly Father wants to be there for us when things are going wrong, but He also wants to be there for us when things are going right.

Just Stuff

Just Playin' Around

I WENT GOLFING A couple of weeks ago, spent an entire afternoon chasing a little white ball all over the place. The weather was great and the company was better ... my game was awful. At least the other guys said that I got my money's worth because I got to hit the ball more times than anyone else. Maybe Mark Twain was right when he said "Golf is a good walk spoiled."

My biggest frustration is that I was rotten at what everyone seemed to find fairly easy. Life is like that sometimes. We look around and think "I wish I was as good a father as ..." or "I wish I was as good a wife as ..." or "I wish I was as good a Christian as ..." The great thing is that we don't have to be. Just as I didn't have to play as well as Ian or Bruce or John, you aren't expected to be like anyone else, only to be yourself.

It's the same when we ask Jesus to become manager of our lives. He doesn't expect us to be a super Christian when we first start to walk with Him; He wants to take us just as we are. Golf takes practice and so does our Christianity!

HAVE YOU BEEN WATCHING the hockey games? I'll admit that I've watched maybe a total of five minutes during the entire series, but my lack of knowledge hasn't prevented me from discussing it with Greg. (That's the story of my life.) In analysing the last game that the Russians lost to the American team, Greg observed that the Russians had more talent but they didn't have the passion. For a minute I thought he was talking about Christians.

We never seem to be lacking in the talent department, there are buckets of it out there. God has blessed His people abundantly with talents and gifts. The question is, "Have we lost the passion, are we missing the fire in our bellies for God's work?" There's a story told about how William Booth, the founder of the Salvation Army, was talking to a man about his soul and the man replied, "If I believed in hell as you do I would crawl across London on broken glass to warn people" I wonder if I would?

In the book of Revelation Jesus condemns the believers in the city of Ephesus for "leaving their first love." I don't know if we've left it or if we've just left our passion for the first love. May our prayer be for the Spirit to re-light the fire in our hearts. After all, our challenge is bigger a hockey game.

SO, HAVE YOU BEEN watching the games? If you have to ask what games then we must presume that you've been occupying another planet. I am not a sports fan, I'm sure that's a surprise to everyone, and even I have been caught up in the hype of the games. Just last week I realized that I was sitting watching curling. Curling!

Stephen, Deborah, and I watched as Herman Maire went sailing through the air in the Men's downhill and watched again as he literally flew down the hill in the giant slalom for his second gold medal of the games. When we see the dedication and determination of these athletes, is it any wonder the New Testament uses athletic competition as an analogy for our Christian lives?

Here's the question then: If Christianity was an Olympic sport, would you finish with a bronze, a silver, or a gold medal? Or for that matter, would you even qualify for the team or would you be relegated to a spectators seat.

What an honour it must be to hear your national anthem played because of your effort. What a greater honour it will be to hear your Saviour say "Well done, my good and faithful servant."

HOW WOULD YOU LIKE to be seven years old and have people comparing you to Wayne Gretzky? In the past two weeks a seven-year-old and an eight-year-old have broken the 104 goal season record that Gretzky set when he was seven. First, seven-year-old Mitchell Davis scored his 105th goal in seventeen games and then, less than a week later, eight-year-old Daniel Luciano scored his 106th goal in the sixteenth game of the season. In contrast, it took Gretzky forty games to score 104 goals.

To be compared to the "Great One" has to be a lot of pressure for a little kid and a fairly heavy mantle to carry. To try to live up to that is going to be tough for both Mitchell and Daniel, because it's not just trying to living up to Gretzky's scoring ability but living up to his character as well.

As Christians we are supposed to be Christ-like, or like Christ, and part of that is living up to His character. I don't suspect that Wayne Gretzky will move in with Daniel or Mitchell to help guide them to their goal, but Jesus' promise to us is that He would send the Holy Spirit for just that reason … to help us to become more like Him.

I CRINGED WHEN I heard about it on the radio. It seemed so, so disrespectful. Just not right. I couldn't believe that it had been allowed to happen, but how do you stop such a thing from happening? In case you're wondering, it was the report that the Stanley Cup fell off a table while on display at a college in Belleville, Ontario. It seemed that a student sat on the table that held the cup and the table flipped under his weight, sending both student and trophy into a pile. It's a terrible thing, but my first thought was, "I hope the cup is all right." It was, and as a matter of interest, so was the student. When I told Greg about the incident, he said that stranger things have happened during its history including having been punted onto a canal and used as a flowerpot.

There used to be a time when I was very careful about how my Bible was treated. I'm probably less conscious of it now. Maybe it needs to become a concern again. If I was dismayed at the treatment of a sports trophy, how much more should the careless use of God's word trouble me?

THEY WERE ROBBED. IT happened in front of thousands of witnesses. You probably saw it yourself. It happened Monday night in Salt Lake City, when Jamie Sale and David Pelletier were awarded the silver medal instead of the gold in pairs figure skating. I can't remember ever being upset over a sporting event in my life, until now. Almost everybody at the Salt Lake Ice Center knew that David and Jamie deserved the gold. I think even the Russian competitors realized that. Sale and Pelletier gave all they had and they skated perfectly. How could first place be given to a team that wasn't as worthy?

It must be a little bit like how God feels, He gave the very best He had, His Son, and we still give Him second place in our lives. What He has to offer is perfect, yet we often award first place to things and people who aren't as worthy. I wonder if that great crowd of witnesses ever looks down at what we have given first place to in our lives and cries out "God was robbed!" They say the Olympic decision can't be reversed, but you can change the position God holds in your life.

Crime and Punishment

LAST WEEK, I SPOKE to a young man who had recently spent two hours playing checkers with Paul Bernardo, surely one of the more interesting ways to spend an afternoon. My curiosity was aroused, so I asked Ray, "What was he like?" The answer shocked me, because Ray said that Paul Bernardo was one of the most pleasant and charming people that he had ever met. He said, "He was the type of guy that you'd want to introduce your sister to." Not the type of personality that we associate with a monster, and if even half of what we read in the paper about the Bernardo case is true, he is indeed a monster.

And again, I was reminded that what is on the outside doesn't always tell the story about what is on the inside. Just as Paul Bernardo attempts to project a very different image than what he is, oftentimes we do the same thing.

Have you allowed Jesus to clean the inside of your life? It's only when that happens that we are able to go through life without the masks we don for society.

WELL, THE BERNARDO TRIAL is finally over. Aren't you thankful that it didn't drag on as long as the Simpson trial? I've gotten so I don't even like referring to orange juice as OJ any more.

Of all the horrific evidence that was heard and seen and written about in the Bernardo case, of all the claims made by his wife and counter-claims made by his defence attorneys, do you know what stuck with me the most? Paul Bernardo had a need to be liked. It was incredible. He was able to admit to some of the most brutal actions that Canadians have heard about in their lives, admit that he kidnapped, terrorized, and violated three teenagers, but he tried to come across as "not a bad guy." It was unreal. Talk about self-delusion.

But I don't know why I was surprised. After all, isn't the common need of men and women everywhere to be liked, no matter how horrible they are? And Bernardo failed. There isn't anyone who likes him, probably not even his parents. Just bring up his name in conversation and listen to the suggestions that people have for Paul Bernardo's fate. He's lucky that his sentence wasn't determined by public opinion.

Christ died for Paul Bernardo, because if Christ couldn't forgive Bernardo He wouldn't be big enough to forgive us.

I READ AN ARTICLE in a national magazine lately entitled "Kids who Kill," and a comment in one of the stories jumped out at me. It dealt with a grade seven boy in Nova Scotia who had used a shotgun to kill a neighbour, apparently without remorse, because he then went home and went to bed.

The thing that caught my attention was that the author of the article was struck by how normal this child was. As I continued to read, though, the boy's father was described as being an abusive alcoholic; the boy was addicted to chewing tobacco, carried a knife everywhere he went, and habitually played hooky from school to hunt and fish. My first reaction was, "Doesn't sound normal to me!"

Maybe I'm naïve, but I thought normal was still parents who weren't abusive and who weren't alcoholics. I would have thought a twelve-year-old boy hooked on chewing tobacco wouldn't have been normal. I would have thought after reading about this boy's background and behaviour that he would have come from one of those dysfunctional families.

It probably serves notice to us that to some people, he was normal and his family was normal. I wonder if the fact that he was a killer seemed normal too! It would seem to be an indication of how big a job we have if the church is going to impact a society where we must be considered to be the oddity. The good news is that no matter how big the job, our God is bigger.

LAST SUNDAY MORNING ON my way down to the office I saw a white pickup driving along the Bedford Highway. Right behind him—and I mean right behind him—was a police car with the lights on, its silly bar flashing and its siren blaring. The guy driving the pickup is meandering along without a care in the world. Later, I got to talk to the officer from the police car and he told me that all he wanted was to get by the guy; he was on his way to another call. In our conversation, the cop told me how frustrated he was that the fellow driving the truck wouldn't even acknowledge that he was there.

I wonder if God ever feels that way with us. You know what I mean? He tries everything to get our attention, and we stroll though life as if we haven't got a care. Throughout the Bible we read of how God got people's attention. Sometimes it was by speaking through his prophets, sometimes He used more spectacular means, speaking through a donkey or a burning bush. Sometimes though, when people constantly ignored God's bidding, it took a tragedy for them to stop and pay attention. The defeats that the Israelites suffered at the hands of their enemies were often wake up calls. I trust that you're open to what God wants for you and are listening to what He wants to say to you.

So, ANYONE CATCH THE story on the news about the guy in Arizona who murdered his wife? Nothing new, if you watch or read the news you realize after a while that people are capable of hurting others, even people they profess to love. Even the method that Scott Falater used to kill his wife, Yarmila, may have been a little extreme, but nothing new. He stabbed her forty-four times and then drowned her in their swimming pool. Ok, maybe more than a little extreme. Even his response was fairly typical; he wore gloves during the crime and hid those and the knife he used in a plastic container in the trunk of his car.

What was unusual about the story? Well, actually, it's the defence that he's using. You see, Falater claims that he was sleepwalking at the time and doesn't remember anything about the incident. That's right, sleepwalking.

As strange as this might sound, people have been fairly creative throughout the years coming up with reasons (excuses) for their behaviour. Maybe they need to read their Bibles because it's quite plain in Psalm 1:5, *"They will be condemned at the time of judgment. Sinners will have no place among the godly."*

Instead of trying to think up excuses, perhaps it's time that we simply admit that we were wrong and need God's forgiveness, even if we did it in our sleep.

HE WAS A FAKE, a fraud, a charlatan. On the other hand he was good at it. Dennis Roark was arrested the other day and could spend up to fourteen years in prison after spending the last four years pretending that he was a doctor. Not just an ordinary doctor, either. Oh no, not Dennis Roark; he aspired to be the very best he could be. As the man said, "Might as well be hung for a sheep as for a lamb." So Roark had been posing as a heart and lung surgeon since 1994.

No patients ever complained about the treatment they received under his care, and there was never any suspicion that he was anything but what he said he was. However, his license to practice medicine in Detroit was suspended after it was discovered in a routine check that he had no medical training. Some people are so picky.

People pretend all the time. They might pretend to be good Christians, or good parents, or good husbands or wives. And even if they pull it off and nobody ever discovers their secret, they know the truth and God knows the truth. Character has been defined as "Who you are when nobody is watching." So, where you at? How would your life stand up to an examination? Maybe it's time to come clean with God and let Him take control and make you all that you're supposed to be and all that you can be.

I WONDER IF HE ever thought about it? Maybe he had simply erased it from his mind, after all, it had been almost thirty years and he must have thought that he had gotten away with it. Who would have thought? I'm sure there were many different reactions to Monday's jury decision which found Larry Fisher guilty of the rape and murder of Gail Miller, a twenty-year-old nursing student. Did Miller's family feel a sense of closure? Did David Milgaard, the man who had been originally convicted of the crime, feel vindicated? Did Larry Fisher feel confused? After all, it looked as if he'd never have to answer for what happened in that Saskatoon alley in January 1969. He's just learned what the Bible taught thousands of years ago when it was recorded in the word of God "and you may be sure that your sin will find you out."

I don't know what is in your history that someday you may have to answer to man for. But the promise of God is that when you ask Him for forgiveness in His eyes your sins are wiped out. That is one great promise.

THEY SAY YOU CAN'T go home. Well Ronnie Biggs certainly proved them wrong. After thirty-six years in exile, he has finally returned home to Britain. Since 1965 Biggs has been on the run from British authorities after escaping while serving a thirty year prison term for his part in the "Great Train Robbery." For the past thirty-one years Ronnie has lived in Brazil, apparently safe from extradition . But the seventy-one-year-old contacted Scotland Yard last week stating that he wanted to return to England and was willing to be arrested at the airport if need be. While it might appear romantic that Ronnie Biggs has chosen to live his remaining days in his native home, he did state that by returning to England he could obtain necessary medical care that he couldn't afford in Brazil.

Deathbed conversions are a lot like that. Someone stated that a deathbed conversion was "Burning the candle of our life for the Devil and then blowing the smoke in the face of God." Being a Christian isn't about avoiding punishment, that's just a perk. Instead, it's about serving a wonderful God and enjoying the blessing He brings to our lives in the here and now as well as the hereafter.

SOME PEOPLE ARE JUST plain nasty, and I'm pretty sure that Michael Wayne McGray fits into that category. The thirty-five-year-old McGray just received his sixth life sentence, this time for the murder of Elizabeth Gale Tucker in 1985. So far McGray has confessed to killing sixteen people across Canada and the United States. After his most recent trial a comparison was made between him and serial killer Paul Bernardo. McGray's lawyer, Wendell Maxwell, made this comment: "I think Michael is in a different class than Bernardo. I think Bernardo was an evil person. Michael, I think, has serious problems." Problems might be one way to describe what motivates Michael McGray, but it's probably not the right way.

Even though we might not be murderers, we are all sinners. Too many of us are guilty of verbal homicide. Our justification for our behaviour isn't much different than McGray's. We have problems, problems with will power, problems with anger, problems with lust, and problems with discipline. But those problems won't be solved until we call them sin, and ask Christ to forgive them and the Holy Spirit to give us victory over them. That will only happen when we really want to be freed from those problems.

Weather You Like
It or Not

HAVE YOU NOTICED HOW windy it's been lately? It seems that every time you catch the evening news, they're either showing scenes of people boarding up windows in South Carolina or Florida, or scenes of destruction throughout the West Indies. By now we all should have become familiar with the hypnotic beauty of the swirling satellite images shown during the weather as well as the meteorologists' assertions that they have no idea what or where the hurricanes are heading. The weather forecasts would almost remind you of the words of Jesus in John 3:8, when he told those following him, *"The wind blows wherever it wants. Just as you can hear the wind but can't tell where it comes from or where it is going, so you can't explain how people are born of the Spirit."*

What Jesus was saying was even though we can't understand the wind, (even today with all of our technological advances) we can't deny its effect or power. In the same way, people may not understand the working of the Holy Spirit in the lives of believers, but they should be able to see the effect and acknowledge His power. After all, one of the attributes in the believer's life is power. If you aren't convinced, just read chapter 1 verse 8 in the book of Acts.

What an incredible rush it would be to see the power of the Holy Spirit unleashed on Metro. That's part of the dream, a dream that can and will become a reality in the life of BCC.

ANGELA AND I WERE marvelling at the autumn colours last week as we drove along the highway. The woods were a kaleidoscope of colours, no two the same. It wasn't hard to imagine Jack Frost painting each leaf individually.

One of the many things we missed during our time in Australia was fall colours. As beautiful and gorgeous and wonderful (have I used enough adjectives yet?) as the weather was in Australia, and it was beautiful and gorgeous and wonderful, their trees didn't change in the fall. To be truthful, I don't think I ever truly appreciated the various hues that paint our forests until they weren't there to see. That's a sad reality of life as well—you don't realize the good you have until you don't have it anymore.

As much as I enjoy the fall scenery I don't appreciate what it takes to make the leaves change—chilly fall mornings leave me cold, so to speak. That's human nature though isn't it? We never seem to want to pay the price, no matter how small. The great thing about the beauty of heaven is that the price has already been paid, and all we have to do is claim it.

HAVE YOU BEEN ENJOYING the weather that we've been having this month? We had one day, week before last, in the high teens and last weekend was absolutely amazing, especially considering that the forecast was calling for heavy rain.

Do you ever think about the weather? There was absolutely nothing we did to deserve the weather we got last weekend. It wasn't payment for something good we had done, we hadn't earned it or bought it, it just came. It was a gift. You ever notice that when we have a hurricane, a tornado, or a killer blizzard, it's an act of God, but nobody calls the weather we had last week a gift of God. Funny, that.

God has another gift He wants you to have. It's called eternal life. You can't earn it, you can't buy it, you didn't do anything to deserve it, it's a gift. The Bible says it best in John 3:16, *"For God loved the world so much that he gave his one and only Son, so that everyone who believes in him will not perish but have eternal life."*

But like any gift it's not yours until you actually take it. I hope you've got yours.

HAVE YOU PICKED UP on the fact that winter isn't my favourite season? As a matter of fact, it doesn't even rank in my list of my top favourite seasons. (They just happen to be summer, summer, summer, and spring.) But it's not just the weather, it's having to listen to everyone gripe about the weather.

When we moved to Australia, I thought that I'd heard the last of negative weather comments. After all, it was said that "In Queensland everyday is perfect, and the next one is better!" But alas it was not to be. People felt the same about the weather down under. It was either too hot or too cold. (Everything is relative. Too hot down there was forty-one and too cold was fourteen.) I wonder if our preoccupation with the weather is actually our attitude toward life, where we are never satisfied with what we have?

Paul wrote in Philippians 4:11 *"Not that I was ever in need, for I have learned how to be content with whatever I have."* Maybe we could add to that "And in whatever province and whatever season!"

HAVE YOU BEEN NOTICING the artistry of God lately? We've had a beautiful autumn and now, as the leaves begin to change colour, I marvel again at the wonder of God's creation. Sometimes we take things like fall scenery for granted. Because we see it every year, it has lost it's wonder.

During the time we spent in Australia one of the things we missed were the splashes of the Master's palette across the forest. Of course one of the things we didn't miss was the cold weather that caused the leaves to change their colours. How human like it is to want to have the benefits without paying the cost. Yet that's the reality of life, everything worth anything costs something.

What are you willing to pay to be a disciple of Christ? How much are you willing to put on the line in your service to Him? The caterpillar doesn't understand what it will take to make him a butterfly. Sometimes we don't understand the process that will make us a committed Christian, but we need to trust that the Master has something beautiful in store for us, even if it does cost a few cold nights.

WELL IT'S OFFICIAL, IT'S here. Honest, it is. Really, would I kid you? Well actually, I would … but not this. After all, this isn't something you kid about.

Summer is officially here, got here at 11:03 last Sunday morning. And all the things that say *summer* are happening; schools out, people traveling, the Sears winter catalogue, hot days. Hot days? Well, almost all the things that say *summer* are happening.

What are your plans for this summer? Are you going away to the cottage? Travelling, going to see relatives? Two things to think about: the first is that I hope you have a great time. In this hectic, hurry-up world that we live in, everyone needs a break. I trust that this will be a great chance to recharge your batteries.

The second thing is that I hope God's included in your summer plans. All too often it is easy to get in the groove of thinking of church and ultimately God as a seasonal activity. You know what I mean. "Well, summer's here, we'll be back to church in the fall." Don't go down that road. Have a great time while you're away but when you're home we'd love to see you and have you worship with us. While you're away, take the opportunity to worship with a church family somewhere along the way. Don't forget, even though it's summer, the bills still need paying so don't forget us while you're gone. I hope you have a terrific summer.

Weather You Like It or Not

WINTER CAME TODAY. I knew it was coming, but I kind of hoped that I was wrong. After all, I've been wrong before. Of course the plans today were to travel to New Brunswick on a ministry trip. What was that line about "the best laid plans of mice and men?"

Where was I? Oh yes, winter came today, I marvel at the fact that, even though winter in Nova Scotia is inevitable, some people still weren't prepared for it. They knew it was coming, I'm sure they didn't seriously think that it would miss us, and yet they were completely unprepared. Tire stores are doing a brisk business either selling winter tires, (I bought mine when it snowed earlier in the month) or installing winter tires that people hastily dug out of their basements.

It's amazing how many people believe in Jesus Christ and believe in the necessity of accepting Him, yet continue to put it off. Don't prepare for winter and you could end up in a ditch. Don't prepare for eternity and you could wind up in Hell. The good news is that you don't have to. Why not take the time today and get things right with your Creator?

WHAT IS IT WITH winter this year? I haven't seen this much snow for years. My driveway is starting to look like a hundred-foot luge run and I'm running out of places to put the white stuff.

However, there are a couple of things to be thankful for, even if you hate winter as much as I do. The first is that, as we get older, this will provide us with the mandatory "bad winter" story to tell our kids and grandkids. "Why, this isn't winter! Why, I remember back in 'oh-one, that was a winter. The snow was clear up to the second story windows." (The depth of the snow is proportional to your age: the older you get, the deeper the snow used to be.)

The second thing we have to be thankful for is that winter doesn't last forever. Even if the groundhog was wrong, spring will be here eventually and then comes summer.

Our Christian life is a lot like the weather. We may not always have sunshine but we have the promise that the rough times won't last forever. Hopefully we won't have to shovel the driveways of our mansions.

Weather You Like It or Not

Spring is here, spring is here, spring is here. I figure maybe if I use the word spring enough, spring will come and warmer weather will spring forth, flowers will spring up, and springs will thaw out. I just looked outside and it seems to be working. Tuesday night during our last bout with winter, my neighbour asked me why I couldn't do anything about the weather and I told her I was in sales not management. (I know, it's not original.)

I'm pretty sure that they taught us in grade two that March 21st was the first day of spring, which makes me wonder what other important stuff they misled me about.

If there is one thing I've learned after living in four countries on three continents, it is that you can't trust the weather. One thing I've learned after having served the Lord for twenty-two years is that you can always trust God. He loves us, cares for us, and has only our very best interests at heart. Regardless of what it's doing outside you can always rest securely on His promises. That ought to add a spring to your step even if the weather doesn't.

ALL I WANT TO know is who ordered the snow? Winter was going along fairly well up until last week, typical Nova Scotia weather, a little snow, a little rain. Then, out of nowhere, we get thirty feet of snow. Ok, maybe I'm exaggerating a little bit ... ok, I'm exaggerating a lot. But still we've had a pile of snow over the past two weeks and I'm getting a little tired of it. Remember, I was the one who voted in favour of global warming. The good news is that spring is just a month and a half away. Regardless of how rotten the winter gets, spring will eventually arrive.

There will be times when it seems we are going through winter in our lives. One storm arrives after another, and it seems that we can hardly catch our breath in between the battering. Don't forget that spring is coming. As sure as day follows night, spring follows winter. Don't give up, hang in and understand that you're not alone. Even when the storms seem to be at their worst, God is still in control, He still loves you, and He wants to be there for you.

Fame

WHAT A WEEK! ON Sunday night we were treated to the Beatles performing together for the first time in over twenty years. On Monday night we were able to find out that, yes, Diana cheated on Charles, but the cur deserved it because he cheated on her first. That has to be expected though, after all it was his father who said "I don't think a prostitute is more moral than a wife, but they are doing the same thing." (These people are at the head of our country, pretty persuasive argument for a republic if I do say so myself.) On Tuesday, people lined up to buy the Beatles' new CD.

Would life ever again be as we knew it? Yes! The Beatles were the group who said they were more popular then Jesus Christ. Well, there were 47 million people watching their second coming on Sunday night. But the Bible tells us in Revelation 1:7 that every one on earth will be watching the second coming of Christ, and that's a pile more then 47 million.

I like the Beatles and I like Princess Di, but how much influence should they have over our lives? Their influence certainly eclipses their importance.

Just a thought, if you've accepted Christ as your Saviour, then you are a child of the King of the universe. That's a whole lot better then being entertainers or a former nursery school teacher.

DID YOU HEAR THE Queen turned seventy the other day? She looks pretty good for her age, don't you think? I mean, considering all she's been through with her kids? I'm not a royalist or a monarchist, but I do think that the lady has gotten a bum rap because of the actions of her children. After all the royal children are all grown ups and QE II can't really be held responsible for their actions. (But you have to admit part of the cause has to be fishing in a murky gene pool.)

Think how much free press we'd get if the newspaper reported every silly thing that our kids did. Do you really think your parents should have had to shoulder all the blame for your brilliance through the years?

She's not the only ruler who cops the blame for their kids' actions. S'truth (by the way, that is an Australian colloquialism for "it is the truth") you think of how much blame gets dumped on God every time one of us pulls a "Duh." There are times that the King's kids don't act any smarter then the Queen's kids do. Well, we might not expect the Windsor children to improve much, but we do have the Holy Spirit to help keep us out of trouble. So let's use His power and show the world the way royalty is supposed to behave!

Fame

MONDAY WAS BILL GATES' birthday. The founder of
Microsoft was forty-one years old. That's only five years older
then I am. At last projection, Forbes Magazine estimated that
Gates was worth 18 billion dollars. That's nine zeros. That's
approximately 18 billion dollars more than I am worth, at least
in a strictly monetary sense. (Greg reassured me that he
wouldn't pay 18 billion dollars for Bill Gates.) That same day I
was reminded that Wayne Gretzky was my age and even
though he is now considered an old man in hockey, (OLD?)
he is one of the greatest players who ever lived.

Sometimes when we start comparing ourselves to the suc-
cesses of the world it's easy to feel a little inferior. Actually, it's
easy to feel *a lot* inferior. But, and it's a big but, dollars and
prestige won't count for much in the eternal scheme of things.
Being the richest man in the world will ultimately pale in
comparison to being a child of God. Although I'd like to have
Bill Gates' money long enough to tithe it for one week. My
prayer is that you have set your sights above worldly wealth
and are looking forward to your reward in heaven.

HAS IT REALLY BEEN twenty years? It hardly seems possible does it? I mean, twenty years is a long time, and it doesn't seem that long ago. Unless you've just arrived on earth, I'm sure that you're aware that we have just commemorated the twentieth anniversary of the death of Elvis Presley. I still remember where I was when I heard the news. Not that you haven't heard that six dozen times. But really that's not all that awesome of an accomplishment. I remember where I was when I first met my best friend in 1974, I remember my first date with Angela, and I remember where I was when I heard that Challenger had crashed.

I also remember where I was September 2, 1979, at 8:30 PM. I was being introduced to Jesus Christ, King of Kings and Lord of Lords. That was the most important introduction in my entire life.

One of Elvis's closest friends tells this story: During one concert a woman placed a crown on the stage at Elvis's feet. Intrigued, he stopped singing, leaned over, and asked her why? She answered, "Because you are the king." Elvis was said to have responded, "No, Jesus is the King, I'm just a singer." Now if the rest of the world would learn that.

My FIRST THOUGHT WAS that I had read the sign wrong. My second thought was that maybe we were thinking of different people. But no, the sign said that the Platters would be performing at a club in Dartmouth. The "Platters" of "Great Pretender" fame, in Dartmouth? However, upon closer examination I discovered that the sign said the "Legendary Platters," not the Legendary "Platters." Legendary was part of the name of the group, not a description of the group. I soon discovered that there are over twenty groups around the world who lay claim to the Platters' name, but there is only one group that actually has a connection to Herb Reed and the original Platters. Needless to say; Herb is a little put out.

Kind of reminds me of Christianity. It's easy to say you are a Christian and all kinds of people do just that. But what connection do you have to the original? The original would be Christ. The Bible warns us that not everyone who calls themselves Christians will be acknowledged by Christ. Only those who obey His commandments actually have a legit claim to His name. How about it? If you call yourself a Christian, do you live up to the billing?

Live and
Let Live

IT'S A FUNNY WORLD! So how come nobody laughs? Did you hear on the news the first of the week that a five-hour-old baby girl was found in the garbage in Toronto? That's not funny, but people's responses to it are. People were outraged. That in itself isn't all that funny either, they should have been outraged. However, when you look at it in the light of 100,000 abortions a year in Canada, if not funny it's at least ridiculous. I think it's wonderful that baby Anne was saved. But doesn't it strike you as peculiar that her life only gained value in the eyes of the law and the media after she had actually been born. Up to that point, she could have been destroyed by her mother with society's blessings and funding from our tax dollars. But, because her mother chose to end her daughter's life two minutes after she was born instead of two minutes before she was born, she was viewed as a monster instead of as a woman simply exercising her freedom to choose.

Aren't you glad that your worth to God wasn't simply dependent on your being born again? The Bible says in Romans 5:8, *"But God showed his great love for us by sending Christ to die for us while we were still sinners."* Even while we were living in disobedience to God, even while we were a nuisance and living in rebellion, Christ loved us enough to die for us. Pretty special huh? Baby Anne could do nothing for her mother and she was left to die. We could do nothing for Jesus, but he came and died for us.

I'M CONFUSED! THAT'S PROBABLY not news to you, but I'm still confused. It's about Brenda Drummond, the woman in Ontario who is being charged with the attempted murder of her unborn son. Now correct me if I'm wrong but, aren't there a pile of doctors in Ontario making payments on their new Mercedes by killing unborn babies? After all, it's been a while since our politicians in their infinite wisdom ruled that it was a woman's right to choose whether or not she wanted to have a baby or kill it in the womb. So with that said and done, I could understand if they were charging the woman with practicing medicine without a license, but attempted murder? Give me a break! Shouldn't she get a rebate from Medicare?

If it wasn't so tragic, it would be funny. Our government has painted itself into a moral corner. It now has to ask itself "If Mrs. Drummond is guilty of attempted murder then what do we do with all our government-funded abortionists? Wouldn't that make them guilty of murder?" And if the doctors who perform the abortions are guilty of murder, what about the politicians who have permitted them to perform abortions?

Can it be wrong for one person to try to kill their unborn baby while at the same time our tax dollars pay for the wholesale slaughter of unborn babies across our country? I think maybe our politicians had better join Mrs. Drummond for her thirty-day psychiatric examination.

SHOULD HE HAVE OR shouldn't he have? There were two people involved. He said he did what he had to do. We'll never know what she thought of the entire thing. The Robert Latimer case is back in the news. I'm sure that you remember the 1993 case where Latimer killed Tracy, his disabled daughter, by carbon monoxide poisoning on the family farm near Wilkie, Saskatchewan. Tracy had suffered from cerebral palsy since birth.

The crux of the debate has been that it has nothing to do with mercy killing or suicide. Tracy was not in pain, nor could she give consent regarding her death. The real issue is whether or not Latimer had the right to kill his daughter for his own convenience. That question could be asked 100,000 times a year as women from coast to coast exercise their right to abortion, which is in reality the right to kill their child for their own convenience.

The question is not one of morality or ethics but of timing, a "Tracy" can be killed in the womb without thought or question, but after twelve years her death can spark a national debate. Well, Tracy's death was wrong, and the 100,000 deaths a year caused by abortion are just as wrong. Not because of timing but because it is the destruction of human life.

So, ANOTHER ABORTION PROVIDER was shot last week. I'm never quite sure how I'm supposed to respond to news like that.

I realize that Dr. Slepian was a husband and a father. I know that he was a human being and that his life was sacred. I'm also aware that the sniper, whoever he was, is in direct violation of the sixth commandment, which says "you shall not murder." I'm aware of all those things, and I stand ready to condemn the shooting of Barnett Slepian as a senseless act of violence. Whoever the shooter is, he has committed a crime that he would undoubtedly justify, just as Moses justified his killing of the Egyptian, (check out Exodus 2:11). But in each case, the sniper and Moses, the killer was guilty of assuming an authority that was not his to assume. Regardless of the shooter's motives, his crime was murder and is to be condemned in no uncertain terms.

But on the other hand … please remember that the victim's name was Barnett Slepian, not Albert Schweitzer. He wasn't a humanitarian. He killed babies for a living. He was and is in direct violation of the sixth commandment, which says "you shall not murder."

Slepian committed crimes that he would undoubtedly justify, just as Moses justified his killing of the Egyptian. But in both cases, Barnett Slepian and Moses, the killer was guilty of assuming an authority that was not his to assume. Regardless of Slepian's motives, his crime was murder and is to be condemned in no uncertain terms.

TWENTY-FIVE YEARS AGO there was a hue and cry in the media about children having children. There was a major concern over the rising rate of teenage pregnancies and what that said about the moral state of our culture. The concern passed as the rate of pregnancy outside of marriage continued to rise, and maybe it really wasn't saying anything about the moral fabric of society after all.

Today there is a hue and cry in the media about children killing children. There is a major concern over the rising rate of murders committed by children and what it says about the moral state of our culture. The tragedy this week is a six-year-old in Michigan who was shot and killed by another six-year-old. That just isn't right.

I wonder—no conclusions here, I'm just wondering—if the moral conditions that could allow children across the US and Canada to violently end the life of another weren't cultivated a long time ago. We cannot discard one section of God's morality and insist on people embracing other parts of it.

Where will it stop? I don't know. I can't speak for society, but to quote a man named Joshua, "But as for me and my house, we will serve the Lord."

I THINK I'D BE a little suspicious and more than a little worried. There was a story in the paper about a couple here in Nova Scotia who are circulating the petition supporting Robert Latimer. As of Monday, they had collected 200 names. I think if I discovered that one of my immediate family members had signed it, I'd be a little suspicious and more than a little worried.

The argument that Latimer used in defence of murdering his twelve-year-old daughter, Tracy, was that it was a mercy killing. His claim was that taking Tracy's life was preferable to her reduced quality of life. It would be interesting to know what Tracey's opinion was of her quality of life. Maybe it was his quality of life that he was worried about.

We all know that Latimer was convicted of his daughter's murder and the Supreme Court of Canada has upheld the conviction, but it's the petitions I wonder about. Are these people concerned about Robert Latimer or are they just laying the groundwork for future actions that they have in mind? I don't know, but it might be worthwhile to check the names on the list just in case.

I READ RECENTLY THAT the B.C. government is seeking to have crimes against abortion providers designated as hate crimes. As usual, I'm a little confused! I would think that most crimes of violence would be by their very nature crimes inspired by hate. While I'm in no way condoning the violence, I wonder if those who are taking part would say, instead of being driven by hatred for the providers, they are guided by compassion for the unborn.

I'm sure their rationale must be that the lives of countless hundreds of children must be more valuable than the life of one doctor. While they may be right, they have not been given the authority to decide who should live and who should die. It's not their decision to make. I'm also confused by the percentage of those people shooting doctors and bombing clinics who profess to being Christians. Did they skip the class where Jesus told us to love our enemies?

The act of abortion itself is a crime of hate: hate directed toward an innocent child who was not to blame and who has no defence. Someday our society will be judged for the Holocaust of abortion, but the answer is not more violence.

WELL, IT LOOKS LIKE Timothy McVeigh won. This past Monday the Oklahoma City bomber had his appointment with the executioner, but he also might have had the last laugh. Probably the worst punishment that could have been inflicted upon McVeigh would have been to lock him away for life. He wanted to die and die he did. Some will think he died a martyr, most will think he died a monster, but he died and that was what he wanted.

With his death came a notoriety that would have been denied him had he simply been locked away. His greatest victory came when three hundred people chose to watch another human being put to death, regardless of how deserving that person was. How far away are we from public hangings or beheadings in the town square? The sad part is that for too many of those who watched, McVeigh's death won't have made it better. Their loved ones will still be gone, their pain will still be present, and a little bit of them will have died while watching the death of another.

Jesus' command to forgive wasn't primarily for the benefit of the forgiven; it was to change the heart of the forgiver.

Holidays, Holy Days, and the Like

Is it my imagination or are there more Christmas lights up this year than there were last year? Angela and I were commenting on it the other night. It seems like every street is trying to outdo the other, at least in Bedford. The displays range from the understated and tasteful to the "Oh my goodness, how do they pay their power bill?" (Check out the place on Basinview just above Bedford Hills Road.)

Everywhere we go there are lights: red lights, green lights, blue lights and clear lights. I even put up lights this year! Christmas truly is a season of miracles. If you haven't seen our tree out in front of the house yet, your Christmas isn't complete.

Now I don't know why people decorate their homes, other than the obvious one that has to do with wives and children, "When are you putting the lights up, huh?" I'm sure that there are a variety of reasons, but the other night as I was driving up Basinview in awe of the work that many people had put into decorating their homes, it dawned on me that whatever the reasons for the lights, the result was that we had decorated for Jesus' birthday. It's like candles on a cake or banners from the ceilings. The people of Bedford, Sackville, Halifax, Dartmouth and the County are shouting out "Happy Birthday Jesus" with their displays of Christmas lights.

Don't forget in all the hubbub and excitement tomorrow to wish your Saviour a happy birthday.

I WAS OUT SHOPPING the other day and came across a cheap bin of Christmas music. Since I've lost my copy of "Cool Yule," I thought "Hey, maybe I can find a copy here." Guess not. But I found a whole bunch of other stuff. "Smokey Mountain Christmas," "R & B Christmas," "Electronic Christmas," "Country Christmas," "Big Band Christmas," and my personal favourite "New Age Christmas." New Age Christmas? Give me a break. On the other hand, the entire world is proclaiming our Saviour's birth this time of year. Stores that would never play "Amazing Grace" play "Away in a Manger." Radio stations that wouldn't know a Christian song if it reared up and bit them are playing "O Little Town of Bethlehem." Surprise, surprise, the most liberal churches around will sing "Round yon virgin, mother and child."

We have to make sure that Christmas isn't the only time of the year that we acknowledge who Christ is. On the other hand, what a great time of the year to say "Hey, I know the Jesus that song is about."

MAYBE I'M A CYNIC. Ok, ok, no maybes about it, I am a cynic. Lately, I've been thinking maybe we ought to give December 25th to the world and let them celebrate their winter festivals or whatever it is they call this time of year so as not to offend anyone.

I know that I've defended Christmas and all of its excesses in the past. I still feel that we should celebrate the birth of Christ. But, does it have to be December 25th? Why not pick a date that is closer to the reality of the Christmas story and celebrate in April or September? I'm sure that we could take Christ out of Christmas and very few people would notice. People would still sing "White Christmas" and "Rudolph," the shopping frenzy would continue, and Santa would still make his trip.

December 25th was selected as a date for Christmas around 270 AD so that the newly converted pagans wouldn't miss celebrating the passing of the winter solstice.

Maybe it's time to return the date to the pagans. After all, they seem to enjoy it the most, and they could once again call it "The birthday of the unconquered sun." The church can throw a private party and celebrate "The Birthday of the Unconquered *Son.*"

FOR EIGHTY-FIVE YEARS he laid in peace, unknown and unbothered. He had lived an unremarkable life, and although his death was a part of history, it was only because of the people he was associated with.

But that has all changed. His tombstone reads very simply, "J. Dawson, Died April 15 1912." In real life Dawson was a stoker on the "S.S. Titanic," an unknown sailor destined for the same obscurity in his death that he had achieved in life.

However, it was not to be. Lately flowers are being laid at the site of his grave in Fairview, not because of who he was but because of who the character Jack Dawson was in the movie "Titanic." I wonder where those people were when they lost a grip on reality. I wonder how long they've operated on the premise that what is on the big screen is reality.

But it's not just moviegoers who mix up fantasy and reality. At this time of the year, people seem to confuse the reason that we observe Easter. It's not to get candy, it's not to provide employment for the Easter Bunny, it's not even to remember the crucifixion. Instead, it is a celebration of the resurrection of the Living God. Let's remember today not what man did on Friday, but what God did on Sunday.

THE EASTER BUNNY IS dead! Well maybe not dead, but it would appear that he may be going the way of the dodo bird and the white rhino.

Maybe you hadn't noticed the subtle change in nomenclature that seemed to be taking place this year. In some malls the egg-laying hare was being referred to not as the "Easter Bunny," but as the "Great Bunny."

Now as far as I am concerned they can call the silly rabbit anything they want to call him, but I really wish that the world would stop hijacking the Holy days of Christianity and trying to make them their own. It's not enough that we've allowed Santa Claus and the Easter Bunny to become a part of the celebration, now they would like Santa and the Bunny to become the celebration. I'm reminded of a cartoon where two women were looking at an Easter display in a store window that included a cross. One of the women comments, "Some people will try to put religion in anywhere."

Last Sunday we celebrated the resurrection of our Lord. That has nothing to do with giant rabbits or chocolate eggs and everything to do with our salvation and eternal life.

So, WHAT DID YOU get your dad for Father's Day? An ugly tie, soap on a rope, or a pair of socks? Luckily it was always your dad who said, "It's not the gift, it's the thought that counts." I trust that you've taken the time to thank your father for everything he's done for you. Or maybe there's nothing to say thank you for.

One of the problems for some people in accepting God as their Father is the memory they have of the way their father treated them. It's unfortunate but true that sometimes the greatest hurts are caused by the ones who are supposed to love us the most. The mere biological act of siring a child does not make a man a father, but listen to how God's word defines our relationship with Him: John 1:12-13 says *"But to all who believed him and accepted him, he gave the right to become children of God. They are reborn—not with a physical birth resulting from human passion or plan, but a birth that comes from God."* Neat, huh?

You see, the truth is this: God isn't necessarily like the father you had, but He is the Father you need.

So Dads, I hope you all have a great Father's Day, and I hope everyone takes the time to thank their heavenly Father for all He is and for all He's done for you.

IT'S NOT THAT FAR away. As a matter of fact it could almost be described as being just around the corner. You know what I'm talking about, even though you are trying to deny it. That's right, "Christmas." It's only forty days away, and if that's not bad enough, there are only thirty-four shopping days left.

Now, I want to take you back to last year. Do you remember all the hustle and bustle that surrounded Christmas? Do you remember all the stress and the things you did that you vowed you would never do again? Can you recall how you resolved that next year would be different? How next year, you would make a conscious effort to make Christ the focal point of Christmas, and how you wouldn't allow yourself to get caught up in all the crass commercialization of Christmas?

Well this is next year. Right now you have the opportunity to make some important decisions concerning how you will celebrate the Christmas season this year.

Take a deep breath. I know you can do it. Now tell yourself, "This year Christ will be the central figure of my Christmas," not Santa, not shopping, not gift giving or gift getting, not the familiar Christmas songs and carols, not even all that wonderful Christmas cooking.

That isn't to say that we do away with all the rest, but let's put all the rest in their proper places. Then we won't have to vow that next year it will be different.

HAVE YOU NOTICED THAT they're not wishing you a "Merry Christmas" in the stores anymore? You might get a "Season's Greetings" or a "Happy Holiday" but woe be upon the poor sales associate who should insensitively bestow upon you a salutation which includes the word "Christmas." The rationale, of course, is that they might inadvertently offend someone from another faith or someone who doesn't celebrate Christmas. Of course, those people aren't offended so much that they refuse to take part in pre-Christmas and post-Christmas sales. That wouldn't be practical would it?

However, the true meaning of Christmas gets the last laugh, because as people push and shove through the crowds to get the very best bargains, the store's public address systems play such words as "Joy to the World! The Lord is come; Let earth receive her King," and "O holy night! The stars are brightly shining, It is the night of the dear Saviour's birth," not to mention "Remember Christ our Saviour, was born on Christmas day, to save us all from Satan's power When we were gone astray."

Maybe our prayer this Christmas should be that people will stop hearing only the tune and truly listen to the message of the Christmas carols, and that God will do a work in the hearts of shoppers all over Metro.

DID I MISS SOMETHING along the way or has the snow-man in "Winter Wonderland" changed from Parson Brown into a Circus Clown? I heard a fairly new sounding version on the radio the other day and thought "What did the poor snowman do to deserve that?" From there I began to speculate on why the change was made. Was it because "Parson Brown" was no longer culturally relevant, because children have so little exposure to church that it would be far-fetched to assume that they would imagine their snowman to be the minister? Or was the question that the snowman asked concerning whether or not they were married ... embarrassing and no longer politically correct? After all, wasn't that question making a value judgment about people's relationships? It shouldn't matter that people are married, and to suggest that the snowman could marry them would imply that they should be married.

Is it guilt that makes people purge even innocent songs of any moral teaching they might have? So another Christmas song has been cleansed, this time not in the name of religious tolerance—heaven forbid that Christmas should reflect Christianity—but in the name of political correctness.

IT'S ALMOST HERE. HOW many of us at one time or another have looked ahead to the year 2000 with almost unbelief? It's always been 1900 and something. Books and movies warned us of what the future would have in store for us, and after we had successfully passed 1984, the only thing we had to look forward to was 2001. (Somehow I doubt that Hal will be there to welcome us.) Regardless of whether or not we thought we'd make it to the year 2000, it's just around the corner. How are you feeling about the dawning of the new millennium? (Don't even start about it not happening until next year.) Are you ready to start writing 00 on all your cheques? I trust that your chequebook is Y2K compliant.

Personally, I'm excited about the New Year, because that's all it really is. We have a brand new year to walk closer with God, a brand new year to tell people about the greatness of Jesus Christ, a brand new year to live in the fullness of the Spirit, and I wouldn't miss it for the world. My prayer for each of you is that 2000 is the best year you've ever experienced as a believer.

Well, we made it through Y2K. At least, if you are reading this, I presume that we made through Y2K. If you're not reading this, either the power grid failed and we couldn't have church, or the entire cyberspace infrastructure collapsed and you can't read it on the Internet. On the other hand, maybe you're not reading it because you just didn't come to church today. Presumably you are reading it, which is good news for Y2K and for your church attendance.

Being only two days into the year 2000 (wow that seems weird) have you had a chance to make and break a few New Year's Resolutions? It seems as if we go into each New Year with the greatest intentions about what we are going to quit or what we are going to start, what we are going to lose or what we are going to find, and what we are going to do or what we are going to don't. Maybe your New Year's Resolution is a spiritual one; you are going to pray more, give more, attend church more, read your Bible more, or tell more people about Jesus. If so, you are going to need help because you already know that you can't do it by yourself. So why not start the New Year by asking God to take complete control.

IT WAS A HOOT. As a family we went to see the movie *The Grinch* this week, and it was great. I may not have approved of everything in the film, but for the most part it was a very funny movie. My favourite line was when Lou Who said "You can't destroy Christmas!" He went on to expound on how Christmas isn't presents and the things on the outside, it's what's on the inside. Of course you know the story, because of the love of little Cindy Lou Who, the Grinch repents and everyone lives happily ever after.

Too often I hear Christians talk about how Christmas is being ruined by this or ruined by that. But Christmas can't be ruined. How we experience Christmas may change for the worse, but Christmas itself will always be a time to celebrate the birth of Christ.

During the next month you will have the option of enjoying the yuletide or allowing people and circumstances to ruin the celebration for you. But whatever you decide, it will be your choice. Wouldn't it be great if your attitude toward Christmas and your love for people caused some Grinch to repent?

So, did you get what you wanted for Christmas? Were all your wishes fulfilled? Were you ecstatic or disappointed on Monday morning? Maybe a little bit of both? I know how you feel. For the fifth year in a row, I didn't have a new BMW convertible in my driveway ... actually, for the fortieth year in a row I didn't have a new BMW convertible in my driveway. But, hope springs eternal. Life often mirrors Christmas in that we don't always get everything on our list. Perhaps the problem lies with our lists.

Maybe we have the wrong wants, except for my BMW of course. So as we move ahead into 2001 (It really doesn't matter what millennium it is, honest!) maybe what we really need to do is make a new list of wishes. I think I'll skip the BMW and instead wish for a deeper relationship with my Lord, a stronger relationship with my wife, and a more authentic relationship with my kids. Instead of just wishing, I think I'll put some effort into it as well, that way there'll be a much better chance the wishes will become reality. Just in case, it would be a 1998 BMW convertible in James Bond Blue.

I HEARD IT AMONGST the hustle and bustle of the season, in the commercial clamour of Sunnyside Mall. My mind was a million miles away as I rushed about my day, and I really wasn't prepared for it, but I heard it anyway. Above the busyness of the day, and through the fog of my daze, the words slowly broke through, "Oh come let us adore him, Christ the Lord!"

One of my favourite things about going into the Christmas season is knowing that for the next month the world will willingly do what they would have problems with the church doing; publicly and loudly proclaiming that Jesus is Lord. Songs of praise and adoration will be sung about Jesus in the most unlikely places by the most unlikely people, and they'll enjoy it. I think that's a hoot. What a great opportunity it is for believers to remind people what they are singing about and what they are celebrating.

The Angel told the shepherds "I bring you good news of great joy for everyone!" 2000 years later the news is still good, the joy is still great, and you will be somebody's angel if you let them know.

TALK ABOUT A SWING in emotions! I have been working on two separate messages this week, one for Good Friday and one for Easter Sunday: a message of despair and a message of hope, a message of defeat and a message of victory, a message about the depths that man can fall and a message about the heights to which God can lift us. Two messages ... both need to be preached but truthfully I prefer Easter Sunday messages to Good Friday messages. I know that without the crucifixion we couldn't have the resurrection, but still ... we killed Him!

He offered us life and we killed him. He came in love and we destroyed Him with hatred. Good Friday? For who? Jesus? They nailed him to a cross. For humanity? We showed how depraved we really can be. Good Friday? I think not. Black Friday? Maybe. Bad Friday? For sure. Without Sunday, Friday is a blot on the history of humanity.

Sunday changes all of that and turns despair to joy, defeat to victory. We may not have been there on Friday, but we are just as guilty. We may not have been there on Sunday, but we are just as forgiven.

WELL, CHRISTMAS HAS COME and gone and New Year's Eve looms on the horizon. How are you feeling about 2002? Are you excited? Are you cautious? Are you simply resigned to it happening?

The reality is that, regardless of how we feel about the coming year, there is a very good chance that it is going to happen, with or without your permission. We have very little control over the coming of the New Year. What we do have control over is how we react to the events of the next 365 days regardless of whether they are good or bad.

Ultimately it will be your choice whether you allow the events that come into your life to make you a better person or a bitter person. Others may determine what happens in your life, but only you will determine what happens in your heart. So, as we bid farewell to 2001 and hello to 2002, let's do so looking forward to the New Year as an opportunity to do great things for God and to allow Him to do great things for us. It's a brand new year with brand new possibilities, if we are only willing to see them and claim them.

Holidays, Holy Days, and the Like

IT MAY BE THIS Christmas' hottest gift. It's not a toy or an electronic gizmo. The two top Bible publishers have reported a surge in Bible sales over the past three months, with an increase of almost forty percent. Citing uncertainty since September 11th and the resulting interest in things spiritual as the reasons for the upswing, it appears that God's word is enjoying a renewed popularity, at least as a possession. It will be interesting to see if more Bibles will actually translate into more people reading the Bible.

The Bible is like any other gift, in order for it to fulfill its potential, it has to be used. If you receive a computer for Christmas and never turn it on, then it's simply a nice paper weight. If you receive a Bible for Christmas and never open it, then it's just a nice book. Even though it may look great on your coffee table and make people think that you have a spiritual side, it won't do what it's supposed to do—change lives, yours in particular. So if you get a Bible for Christmas this year, take the time to read it. It will change your life.

WELL, A NEW YEAR is upon us. 1997 is now nothing but a memory and 1998 is stretched out ready for us to make our mark. Got any plans for the new year? Are you planning on starting some new habits or ditching some old ones? 1998 could be the year to do it.

As we came to the end of December, the thought came to me, "This could be the year the Lord returns." You know, there was a time that event was seen as imminent; the thought and hope in believers hearts and minds was "perhaps today." I wonder if we've gotten too comfortable in this old world? I wonder if we've lost the desire to dance on streets that are golden and are content to drudge along on streets that are asphalt?

I am in no way advocating that believers not prepare and plan for the future. I'm just saying don't forget, He said He would be back, and He will be back. Ten years ago I received a book in the mail entitled "88 reasons why Christ could return in '88." Well He didn't but He could have. I trust that 1998 will be a great year for each of you. May you be able to say, as did the early Christians, "Maranatha," which means "Come O Lord!"

That's Just Funny

HAVE YOU EVER LOST control? I mean really lost control? The other night after Angela and I went to bed we lost control. No, not that way! It was our temperature. She told me that no matter how high she turned her electric blanket control she was still cold! I thought that was funny because no matter how low I turned my control I was still hot! That's a no-brainer isn't it? We had the blanket on upside down, and we were controlling each other's side. The colder she got, the higher she turned her heat, and the hotter I got, the lower I turned my heat, and the colder she got. The solution of course was to get out of bed and flip the blanket over. If only the solution to all of life's problems were as simple.

Maybe they are! Maybe the problem is the same one that Angela and I had, a matter of trying to control that over which we have no control. There are things in life that we have no control over, and we need to leave those things to God.

Jesus Christ told us in Luke 12:25-26, *"Can all your worries add a single moment to your life? And if worry can't accomplish a little thing like that, what's the use of worrying over bigger things?"*

We aren't losing control when we give those things that we can't control anyway over to God. We're simply delegating it! And all good managers will tell you that once we delegate something … we shouldn't take it back.

MY AUNT CALLED MY eighty-nine-year-old grandmother a couple of weeks ago and asked what she was doing. The reply was a little disconcerting because my grandmother replied, "Just sitting on the couch waiting for the undertaker." Well, Aunt Bernice could hardly believe her ears. "I beg your pardon", she said. So my grandmother repeated herself, "Just sitting on the couch waiting for the undertaker." My aunt was a little upset and began to lecture my grandmother on not giving up and how healthy she was and that she couldn't take a defeatist attitude toward life. When Bernice was finished my grandmother responded by saying, "I don't know why you're so upset. Neil called and said he was dropping over this afternoon." In case you haven't figured it out, Neil is a great-grandson who just graduated from funeral director's school.

However, there are a lot of people out there who are "just sitting on the couch waiting for the undertaker," and they don't even know Neil. I trust that you have decided to live life and to live it to its fullest. Jesus said in John 10:10, *"My purpose is to give them a rich and satisfying life."* Jesus didn't promise us just a little bit of life, he promised us abundant life, and we'd be fools not to take it. So let's stop waiting for the undertaker and start living like overtakers, because life is ours for the taking.

That's Just Funny

THE NOISE WOULDN'T STOP, and it was getting a little annoying. We were going out to dinner last Monday and before we had travelled very far the noise started and it just wouldn't stop. Angela asked why the car was making the funny noise. I told her it was probably a combination of the rain, the wind, the fan being on high, and Deborah's music coming from her Discman. The last thing I needed was more car repairs, and I was kind of hoping that if I refused to acknowledge the noise it might go away by itself. But it wouldn't stop and it was getting a little annoying. Well, imagine my surprise when we stopped to pick up Angela's father and she discovered my neighbour's trash can under my front bumper. Boy was my face red. But no harm was done … well, except to the can. We all had a good laugh and our neighbours got a nifty new trash can.

Sometimes, though, ignoring warning signals in our lives can have worse consequences than a dead trash can. Is it any wonder that the Bible commands us not only to listen to God, but to pay attention?

I LOCKED MYSELF IN the trunk of my Ford the other day. Of course it wasn't an accident, how dumb do you think I am? (By the way, that was a rhetorical question and doesn't require an answer.) It was on purpose. The latch wasn't latching and the only way I could see what the problem was, was from the inside. So, I put my keys on the roof, put my cell phone in the trunk with my tools, crawled in and fiddled until I got it working. At that point I was locked in the trunk of my Ford. But not to fear, I had my cell phone and I called my daughter, who was inside watching television. After several minutes of explanation she came and rescued me. However, as I started to dial, a couple of thoughts went through my mind: what if the reception inside the trunk is rotten and it won't connect? What if Deborah's on the phone and I get a busy signal? Luckily as Christians, that's not a concern in connecting to God. Our promise as believers is found in Psalm 91:15 *"When they call on me, I will answer; I will be with them in trouble. I will rescue and honour them."*

IT WAS ONLY A small mistake. I mean, I was only off by one. It shouldn't have mattered that much, but it did. Although not overly gifted with a mechanical aptitude, I do occasionally venture under the hoods of our cars. Just last week I changed the rotor button and distributor cap on the Ford. Knowing how important the firing order was, I very carefully moved the wires from one cap to the other. I was so proud of myself until I tried starting the car and it absolutely refused to go—didn't even try to go. I wasn't frustrated. Not much anyway.

Actually, I was really frustrated. I tried it three or four more times and it still wouldn't go. It was only after I found the firing order and then noticed the numbers on the wires that I realized that I must have had the new cap turned when I so carefully matched up the wires. But I was only off by one, eight times.

In our Christian life we can often justify an action as only being a small mistake. How often does that small mistake multiply itself to have major consequences? Maybe like the car, the easiest way is to get it right the first time.

THE OTHER NIGHT AT the pool I ran into a man and his three-year-old daughter whom I had met on one other occasion. They left before I did and as I was preparing to leave I noticed he had left his daughter's life jacket beside the hot tub so I picked up the life jacket and threw it in my bag. I had an idea where they lived and so made my way to their home in the rain; after all it was a dark and stormy night. Imagine his surprise when I showed up at his door and said, "Hi, I brought your daughter's life jacket back." Imagine my surprise when he said, "That's not my daughter's life jacket!"

Driving the extra twenty-five kilometres in the rain to return the life jacket to the pool hadn't been on my agenda for the evening, but it goes to prove that no good deed goes unpunished.

I felt kind of silly on his doorstep and even sillier at the pool explaining where I got the life jacket and why I was bringing it back. But I did it for the right reasons, and I hope that the fear of feeling silly won't ever keep me from trying to do the right thing.

That's Just Funny

When You're Dead, You're Dead

IT'S 1998.
YOU'RE DEAD.
What do you do NOW?

What a great question. What a great ad. It was in this week's TIME Magazine and it was sponsored by the "Life and Health Insurance Foundation for Education." Maybe the church ought to run the same ad. After all, insurance is talking about your family being comfortable for a few years after you're gone, and the church is talking about people being comfortable for an eternity after they're gone.

How would you answer the question from a spiritual perspective? It's 1998. You're dead. What do you do now? Is it going to be heaven or is it going to be hell? The great thing is … it's your choice. Nobody else can send you to either place. It has to be your decision. The word of God says in the book of Deuteronomy 30:19, *"Today I have given you the choice between life and death, between blessings and curses. Now I call on heaven and earth to witness the choice you make. Oh, that you would choose life, so that you and your descendants might live!"*

ERMA BOMBECK IS DEAD! I couldn't believe it when I heard it two weeks ago. It was almost like losing a friend. My mother first introduced me to Erma when I was a teenager. I didn't actually meet her in person, I met her through her book *The Grass is always Greener over the Septic Tank*. From that book on I was hooked on Erma. For years she kept me laughing and taught me that we shouldn't take life too seriously because we'll never get out of it alive.

My first thought when I heard the news was there won't be anymore books. My second thought was how could someone so young be dead. She was sixty-nine and I could hardly believe that. After all, she was only in her forties when I began reading her books as a teen.

A bigger shock then her death was how little was made of it. There was a short little column in the paper, a blurb on the radio, and a couple of seconds on the television. It somehow doesn't seem fair that someone who brought so much joy into people's lives could be dismissed almost out of hand. I wonder how much press Sadaam Huessein will get when he dies? I don't care about how much press I get when I go, but I do hope there will be folks out there who say "He had an impact on my life."

Thanks, Erma, for making me a better person.

FIVE PEOPLE DIE A violent death in Los Angeles every day, thirty-five a week, over two thousand a year. For the most part they are all nameless individuals who die in drug-related killings or drive by shootings. Oh, we know that L.A. is dangerous but it never seems to intrude into our world. That all came to an end last Thursday when Ennis Cosby, the only son of Bill Cosby, was shot and killed while changing a tire. I'm sure that many people had problems realizing that it was Ennis Cosby who died and not Theo Huxtable.

Our hearts go out to the Cosbys during this time of tragedy, but it certainly brings home the fact that not everyone in this world is treated equally. Twenty minutes after CNN started broadcasting video images of the murder scene and victim, they discovered who it was and stopped, because of the intrusion into the Cosby's grief. Would that have happened for Corrie Compton murdered the same day? Within days, two major publications and the city of L.A. offered a $312,500.00 reward for Cosby's killer. Would that have happened for Corrie Compton? L.A. Mayor Richard Riordan was calling the Ennis Cosby murder "Priority number one." Would that have happened for Corrie Compton? The only person who seemed to remember Corrie was Bill Cosby, who expressed his concern and grief to her parents.

Isn't it great, though, to know that regardless of who we are or who we know, that we are God's number one priority?

My Grandmother died last week. On Sunday we made a flying trip to Grand Manan Island to attend the funeral, and it was quite a celebration. You have to keep in mind that Gram was almost ninety years old and had served the Lord for most of those ninety years. As a high school student I was intrigued with the words of John Donne, who wrote "One short sleep past, we wake eternal, and Death shall be no more: Death, thou shalt die!" As an unbeliever I didn't understand it. As a Christian I claim it; this weekend I saw it. Part of my grandmother's testimony had to be in the fact that they had to figure out how to include the three grandsons, one great-grandson and a grandson-in-law who were pastors in the service. Each one of us had been prayed for and influenced by a godly grandmother.

Rumour has it that John Wesley once remarked, "Whatever else the world might say about we Methodists, they have to admit, we die well." Gram may not have been a Methodist, but she died well.

The question then is "Will you die well?" Only you can answer it. The answer can only be found in the one who said, *"I am the way, the truth and the life, no one comes to the Father except through me"*

WELL, GENE RODDENBERRY, THE creator of Star Trek, has now bravely gone where no man has gone before—at least no dead man. This past Monday the cremated remains of Roddenberry, along with the ashes of hippie guru Timothy O'Leary and twenty-two others, were sent into space aboard a Pegasus rocket as the first-ever space funeral. You gotta admit though ... it probably made more sense than the group from "Heaven's Gate."

I'm sure that people who work out in great detail what is to be done with their remains are trying to somehow extend their influence from beyond the grave. They feel that if they can still be in control when they are gone then they have won the battle.

Well, you can put me out with the recyclables when I'm gone because Jesus has already won the battle for me. It has nothing to do with this shell we call a body. It was Paul who wrote in 1 Corinthians 15:55-57, *"O death, where is your victory? O death, where is your sting? ... But thank God! He gives us victory over sin and death through our Lord Jesus Christ."*

WELL, SHE'S DEAD! BUT she certainly had a good run of it. 122 years, 6 months, and 18 days after she was born, Jeanne Calment died. She was officially the oldest woman in the world. Actually, she was the oldest living human on the planet at the time of her demise. From all accounts Jeanne Calment lived a full life, a life that she enjoyed.

We all have something in common with this lady: each one of us has one life to live. It may have 122 years in it or less then half of that, but each of us has one life. We have no say in how long or how short that life will be, but each one of us will determine how full or how empty our life will be. The secret, you will remember, is not how many years you get in your life but how much life you get in your years. In John 10:10 Christ promised us a life full to the point of overflowing, and that promise is for every believer. The trick though is to do your part. You see, Jesus may promise you an abundant life but it won't do you any good unless you are willing to live that abundant life. And that my friend can only be decided by you. So what's it going to be, a full life or an empty life? It's up to you.

ONCE UPON A TIME in a faraway kingdom there lived a beautiful princess who was loved by everyone, not only in her kingdom but in other kingdoms as well. She was kind and gentle, and people loved to see her and to hear about her loves.

In the same kingdom there lived a playful dragon named "Grog." Many of the people of the kingdom enjoyed playing with Grog even though he had a few annoying habits. Sometimes Grog had been known to get carried away and hurt the people he played with, sometimes families were destroyed, and sometimes people were killed. Oh well.

One day the beautiful princess and her love had been to a banquet, feasting and making merry. What they didn't realize is that one of her love's servants had brought along the playful dragon. To make a long story short, in his own unique way, the dragon managed to destroy the beautiful princess, her love, and her love's servant.

The people of the kingdom loved their beautiful princess, but because they enjoyed playing with Grog, they didn't want to offend the playful dragon by blaming him or, heaven forbid, by banishing him from the kingdom. So they sought to blame her love's servant and the peasants who followed her about. Nobody lived happily ever after. Except maybe the dragon.

(This was written concerning the death of Princess Di.)

"*THIS IS WHAT JESUS came to teach us, how to love, how to love one another.*" I watched an hour long special on the life of Mother Teresa the other night, and she used that phrase over and over again. If her life was any indication, it was a lesson that the little Albanian nun had learned very well.

In listening to people's reactions to the death of Mother Teresa I have become convinced that the King has had no greater ambassador over the past seventy years than this lady. While the Roman Catholic Church has a fairly strict set of guidelines that they need to follow before Sainthood can be bestowed upon Teresa, it would appear that it has already been done by the majority of the Christian world.

Jesus was fairly clear when he said in John 13:35, "*Your love for one another will prove to the world that you are my disciples.*" Mother Teresa's love for the poor of the world was evidenced not only in her words but, more importantly, in her actions. The world will be a poorer place without the love of Mother Teresa, but I'm sure that she's enjoying being in the presence of the one she served so faithfully throughout her life.

When You're Dead, You're Dead

SONNY BONO IS DEAD! Now the reality is that celebrities die all the time, but Sonny was different, he was someone who came into our living room once a week as I was growing up. If Sonny and Cher weren't family, they were at the very least regular guests. Now Sonny is dead.

He was an entertainer, a television star, and lately a successful politician, and now he is dead. The victim of an accident, nobody's fault. Sonny died just like we are all gonna die; it may not be an accident, it may not happen someplace as pretty as Lake Tahoe, but you are all going to die.

I have no idea where Sonny Bono will spend his eternity, and it really isn't all that important to me, but you can rest assured that he will be spending it somewhere. On the other hand, I do care about where you will spend your eternity, so I have to ask, do you care about where you will spend eternity?

If they were to find you dead on a ski slope tomorrow morning, or in your driveway, or in your bed, do you know where your soul would spend forever?

I SAT IN STUNNED silence; I couldn't believe what I had heard. It was as if I had lost someone I knew, yet it was just a name. The news that Pierre Trudeau's youngest son had been killed in an avalanche while hiking in British Columbia hit me like a ton of bricks. I hadn't thought of Michel Trudeau in years, probably since he was a toddler and his dad was in the news on a regular basis, and yet I remember gasping, "Oh no!" when I heard. How come? There are a couple of reasons. First, I was a major Trudeau fan during my teen years (much to my father's chagrin). The grief I felt was less for Michel and more for the pain that his father was going through. To say Pierre Trudeau had a major impact on who I am might not be complimentary but it is true, and I was sad that a man who held a important place in my memory was grieving.

The other reason is that I was reacting as a parent. The thought of losing a child is almost unbearable. After all children are supposed to bury parents, parents aren't supposed to bury children. The pain of having a child die, whether by disease or accident, must be horrific. So again the words of John 3:16 seems like an even greater miracle. John 3:16, *"For God loved the world so much that he gave his one and only Son, so that everyone who believes in him will not perish but have eternal life."*

When You're Dead, You're Dead

I REMEMBER WHERE I was when I heard the news; it happened this past Sunday morning around six while I was canoeing. It was quite a shock, even though I knew it was going to happen. It seems like he's always been a part of my life, maybe only in a peripheral way, but he was still a part of my life. Of course I'm talking about the death of Charles Schultz. After the news had registered, I had this mental image of Schultz in heaven and a long line of people were waiting to tell him what their favourite "Peanuts" cartoon had been.

Most of us may not have a line waiting in heaven to congratulate us on our earthly achievements, but won't it be great if there is a line of people to greet us whose eternity we had impacted? I believe that one of the ways you will be able to have an eternal impact on someone's life will be through the "Power to Change" campaign. There's a list of training venues and times in the bulletin, take a look. After all, three hours on your part might just mean eternity for somebody else. Oh, by the way ... I read the news at www.canoe.ca.

I EXPECTED IT, BUT it still came as a shock. Pierre Elliot Trudeau was the first politician to hold my interest as a child and perhaps the last politician to hold my interest as an adult. And now he's gone. Love him or hate him, you have to admit that he had a profound impact on our country and, with the possible exception of John A. MacDonald, was the strongest prime minister to ever lead Canada. It was Trudeau who brought both official languages into fashion, who showed his strength during the October Crisis of 1970, who brought the constitution home in 1982, and who gave us an incredible national debt. Any one of those things will keep him in the history books, but they matter not an iota today.

All that matters in the end is whether or not Pierre Elliot Trudeau accepted the grace and forgiveness that Jesus offers. All of the flags flying at half-mast, all of the roses left behind, and all of the dignitaries' words will pale in comparison to being able to hear Jesus say, "Well done my good and faithful servant." We don't know if Trudeau accepted that gift; the important question is have you?

When You're Dead, You're Dead

HE WAS TWENTY-FIVE when the First World War broke out and fifty when the Second World War started. When he was seventy-four JFK was assassinated, and the year he turned eighty Neil Armstrong walked on the moon. He saw the advent of automobiles, television, and computers and lived in three different centuries, but now Benjamin Holcomb is gone. Holcomb, an Oklahoma farmer, died this past week at one hundred and eleven years of age; he had been the world's oldest living man. Most of us won't live to be a hundred and eleven but we are still responsible for the years we have, whether they be long or short. The secret for living isn't how many years we get in our life but how much life we get in our years. The secret for dying is completely different. It has nothing to do with the impact that your life will make on the world and everything to do with the impact Christ's life made on yours.

Ben Holcomb lived one hundred and eleven years on this earth, but where he'll spend his eternity was decided by whether or not he embraced the salvation that only Christ can give. Like Benjamin Holcomb, our eternity will depend on a decision only we can make.

It's the Law

IT'S A TOUGH CALL! When do you stand up and say "enough is enough?" What are we getting into with the new legislation enshrining the rights of homosexuals? I don't think that homosexuals should be discriminated against. But (and you know that after the *but* comes the truth,) will the new legislation give them special protection? Could we as a church refuse to hire an adulterer because of religious convictions but be forced to hire a homosexual because his or her rights had to be protected? Inquiring minds want to know.

I don't think that homosexuals are a special breed of sinners who we need to be protected from. On the other hand, I would hope that the laws that are in place currently would provide them with the same protection that I have as an evangelical Christian, which probably isn't that much, come to think about it.

Where do we stop? If homosexuals need protection from discrimination, what about fat people, or ugly people, or fat, ugly people ... probably the most discriminated-against block of Canadians there is.

It's funny how we treat sin. First it's denounced, then it's ignored, then it's tolerated, finally it's protected.

I WENT THROUGH A speed trap last week. Actually, I went through two speed traps on the same day, and I have to confess I was speeding both times. (I know you'll find that hard to believe but it just confirms Billy Sunday's words, "Sin can be forgiven, but stupid is forever.") The relief I felt when the car behind me was pulled over probably wasn't shared by the other driver, and I actually thought "what a selfish feeling."

My rationale for not getting caught was that I was staying less then ten percent over the speed limit. It was a conscious thought. My cruise control was set for 109 kilometres per hour because they usually don't stop you if you're going less then 110. The fact of the matter is that I was still in the wrong. After the second instance of getting my heart out of my throat I thought, "I wonder how often in life we justify ourselves as only sinning ten percent?" "I know the limit but I'm just a little over it." But sin is still sin and disobedience is still disobedience. You can't be partly disobedient any more than someone can be partly pregnant ... "you either is or you isn't" ... there's no middle ground.

God doesn't call us to partial obedience, and He doesn't expect us to stay within a ten percent margin. God expects His children to be obedient, and He can provide us with what it takes to be obedient. I wasn't speeding because I couldn't help myself. I was speeding because I wanted to, and I deserved a ticket. I bet God would be tickled pink if we as His children wanted only to be one hundred percent obedient to His will.

It's the Law

I THINK I SEE the problem. It's all becoming clear after a recent article I read concerning Howard Epstein's objection to the Lord's Prayer being recited in the provincial legislature. Epstein stated, "If people want to pray, let them pray either in private or in their houses of worship." That isn't where I see the problem. I'm not sure I see the value in a bunch of bored politicians mumbling their way through the Lord's Prayer simply because they have to. Somehow I think that has to fall into the category of prayer that Jesus referred to as "vain repetition." The problem, I think, can be found when Epstein said his main objection was to the concept of politicians praying.

Now there's a concept … or a lack of one. Perhaps, just perhaps, our politicians haven't been praying enough, either inside the legislature or outside. We've seen what they can accomplish on their own, maybe a little outside help from the Almighty is called for. Couldn't hurt! If all the Christians who will be outraged over the suggestion of removing the Lord's Prayer from the legislature had been praying for the legislature, then maybe that would have made a difference too.

I FOUGHT THE LAW and the law won. I've known the words to the song for years but only recently have I felt the emotion. Yes, your pastor is nothing more than a common criminal. It all began innocently enough, I knew it was wrong but somehow I was able to justify it to myself. Then I did it again and again; I was out of control. But it's all over now, last Friday night the long arm of the law reached out and nabbed me. Now there's nothing I can do but suffer the consequences. All along I knew there would be a price to pay but I thought the benefit would outweigh the penalty.

That's right, I parked our Ford on the street during last week's snowstorm and ended up with a $15.00 ticket. When I started that nasty habit I decided that if I got ticketed, and I didn't think I would, that the ticket would be worth the aggravation of having my car stuck in my driveway. I was wrong.

The Bible says that obedience is better than sacrifice; the snowplow driver who reported my car must have felt the same way. There are people who disobey the Word of God thinking that the price will be worth the pleasure. It won't be.

It's the Law

IT WOULD APPEAR THAT, without a consensus from the business community, the Nova Scotia government is going to defer a sticky issue for at least four more years. The headlines of this morning's paper read "No Sunday shopping before 2005." Justice Minister Michael Baker said that without consensus it remained up to the government to make the decision, which it did. It is kind of interesting to note that while the newspaper did refer to Sunday as the Sabbath a couple of times (and we're not getting into that debate), there was no mention of the spiritual element of the day. I guess it's just a day that a lot of people have off. Somewhere along the way Sunday has been transformed from a holy day to a holiday.

Now before we get on our high horse about that, let's admit that it's not a whole lot different for most Christians. For too many believers, Sunday's spiritual element has to be contained somewhere between 10:00 AM and noontime. Outside of that time frame we feel free to eat out, buy whatever we need, watch the kids play hockey, or even catch a movie. Perhaps if Christians took the Lord's Day a little more seriously, everyone else might too.

TOM GREEN SAYS HE'S just being true to his faith and what his religion requires. Dave Leavitt, however, says that Green is a criminal and, as a prosecuting attorney, is trying to put him in jail. The reason? Leavitt says that what Green is doing "hurts society." No doubt about it, what Tom Green is doing is wrong, morally and legally. The man has five wives and twenty-six children. But to claim that his polygamy hurts society? Is Leavitt actually convinced that a fifty-two-year-old man living with five women and their children in a collection of trailers in the remote desert of Western Utah is a threat to our society? A society where you can marry and divorce as often as you like, where homosexuality is considered to be just another valid life style choice, where abortion is seen as a right? This is the society that Tom Green's going to hurt. What the man is doing is sin, and he needs to repent, but I don't think his actions have much chance of hurting society. It was Mark Twain who stated that the Bible was against bigamy, after all, Jesus did say, "no man could serve two masters."

It's the Law

That's Life!

MY COMPUTER DIED ON Wednesday. As a matter of fact, this could be the first time that the "Penn of Denn" was actually written with a Penn! Have you ever noticed how you don't realize how much you depend on something until it's gone? Like when your car or second car breaks down and all of a sudden you're trying to cope with fewer wheels. In August when we relocated the office we were without phones for three weeks. I never thought I'd miss my phone but I did. This past week it was like my best friend had left me.

What would happen if God removed Himself from our lives for a couple of days? Would that be what it takes for us to realize how dependent we are on Him?

Without my PC I was reduced to communicating with pen and paper, when we didn't have our phones we needed two cans and a piece of string, when the LeBaron breaks down I have to walk, but where would we be without God?

ANGELA'S CAR DEVELOPED A little bit of a shimmy in the front end last week. To call it a little bit of shimmy is like calling the Atlantic Ocean a little bit of water. You could hardly hold on to the steering wheel, it was shaking so bad. Now the Crown Victoria isn't a little car, so I figured it had to be something major to shake a car that big. Not! The mechanic showed me the bulge on the bottom of the tire that was causing the problem. It was big as far as bulges go, but it wasn't very big in relation to the size of the ark Angela drives.

Sometimes it doesn't take very much to shake up our lives. You've been there. One minute you figure you have everything under control and the next thing you know, you can hardly hang on. The problem is that often we suspect that it's something major when in reality it may be something simple, just not obvious. Maybe it's time to check for the little things that are throwing our lives out of balance. Maybe it's time to stop trying to fix it ourselves and time to ask the Holy Spirit for some help.

That's Life!

DON'T YOU JUST LOVE irony? Last week you may remember I wrote about what I thought was going to be a major problem with Angela's car, and it turned out to be a minor problem. Two days later I took the car back to the mechanic for what I thought was a minor noise, maybe the new tires were out of line? Instead of being a minor problem, we ended up replacing the entire rear end of the car. Can you say "expensive?"

In retrospect I would rather have a problem I thought was big and turned out to be little then the other way around.

The danger is there spiritually as well. How often has it been that what was perceived as a little problem has trashed a person's Christian witness? I didn't catch the problem with the car because the noise had started small and I grew accustomed to it when it should have been a warning signal. I hope we don't tune out spiritually to some of the warnings given to us by the Holy Spirit. Remember, it was Jesus who said *"He who has ears let him hear."*

WELL, I FINALLY BROKE down. After tiptoeing through the snow, slush, and water for a month, I decided it was time I went ahead and bought a pair of winter boots. With that in mind and the very best of intentions, I ventured forth Tuesday night to procure said footwear. But as I got closer to the shoes and boots, I began to experience a strange sense of deja vu. Finally I turned to Angela and said, "I think I bought a pair of winter boots last year." Once we got home I checked in the hall closet. Sure enough, there were my boots. (Do you ever think to your self "Denn needs a vacation." Maybe something in the line of a Caribbean cruise?)

How often do we live like that as Christians, never clueing in to the fact that the things we think we need have already been provided for us. Listen to what Paul says in 1 Corinthians 4:8 (NIV), *"Already you have all you want! Already you have become rich! You have become kings ..."* What a great promise. Don't confuse it with paltry material wealth. Instead, realize that His promises are greater then the things of this earth. Like my winter boots, they are already ours.

That's Life!

DO YOU LIKE CHEWING gum? Stephen, my son, my eldest child, has been chewing the same piece of gum for a month! Not continuously mind you, he does take it out to sleep, to go to school, and to eat … but then … back in it goes. Now, when queried about this phenomenon, he replied that he was trying to set a record. To be truthful, I didn't know there was a record for chewing one piece of gum the longest, but then again I'm only an adult.

The reality is that the flavour in Stephen's gum is gone, whatever enjoyment was there to begin with is missing now, and the gum is chewed by rote.

I wonder how much Stephen's gum chewing is like some people's Christian experience? Once it was fresh and wonderful, full of flavour. But as time has marched on it has lost its flavour. Now it's just something you do, not necessarily something you enjoy. Has your Christianity become more of a personal habit instead of a personal experience? Does this describe your walk with God? Stephen needs a new piece of gum. Do you need a new touch from the Lord?

TUESDAY EVENING ANGELA AND I went out to dinner to celebrate our eighteenth anniversary (we married very young) and ended up feeling queasy. It must have been the jalapenos.

4:30 Wednesday morning I woke up hearing a dripping noise from the bathroom. Upon further investigation, I found the drip coming from the ceiling. Later that morning Angela called to tell me the water in the bathtub wouldn't drain. I obviously have a directionally challenged home.

That afternoon a man came to inspect our van, which is at the end of its lease, and he told me that it was going to cost me almost $600.00 to replace the winter tires. Oh well, at least I still have my twelve-year-old Ford. What a week, and it's only Wednesday. To think, all I have to look forward to next week is turning forty!

But on reflection, life could be a whole lot worse. God is still on His throne and we have much to give thanks for.

You know, it's not that bad, our contractor is coming to fix the leak, liquid plumber fixed the drain, and I can put used tires on the van and it will only cost me $200.00. Now if I could only find out what to do about turning forty!

That's Life!

THE PEOPLE WERE PARTING before him like the Red Sea before Moses. If you missed the picnic on Sunday then you missed the excitement. Diesel, our 140-pound Great Dane slipped his lead at Oakfield Park and made a break for it. It only took five minutes to catch him, but that gave him the chance to run through every group at the park. We were trying to catch him for his own good, but that wasn't the way he saw it, he thought we just wanted to ruin his fun. Do you ever slip your lead and run from God? You're sure that the guidelines that He has put in place are only there to ruin your fun, but He knows they are there for your protection.

One of the frustrating moments as we endeavoured to get Diesel back was when a lady yelled, "Put a leash on that dog!" Duhhhh, what did she think I was trying to do? There are times that people wonder why God doesn't put a leash on Christians. It would make life a whole lot easier. The reason I didn't leash the dog was that I couldn't catch him ... the reason God doesn't leash us is the gift called free will.

WHAT A BEAUTIFUL WEEKEND we had last week! I took the opportunity of the great weather to paint the window frames on the second storey of our house. It wasn't a big job, but I dislike painting and I hate heights, so when you put them together it was a job I had been putting off all summer. I think the high point came when our Great Dane wrapped his lead around the bottom of the ladder while I was at the top of it. Now I love that dog, but I got a little distracted from what I was supposed to be doing while I was watching him do what he thought he was supposed to be doing. So I had to put him inside the house.

In my spiritual life, I have discovered that when I finally get around to doing the things I should be doing, there are always distractions that pop up to keep me from finishing the job, and I understand what Paul meant when he wrote *"I want you to do whatever will help you serve the Lord best, with as few distractions as possible."* What's distracting you from doing your best for Him?

I HAD A BIRTHDAY last week. Yes, another year older. Another year away from birth, another year closer to the grave, not that it bothers me. I'm not ashamed of my age. As a matter of fact, I'm down right proud to be thirty- seven.

It's all relative, isn't it? Maybe you're old enough to remember when the cry was to not trust anyone over thirty. Thirty? That same generation now tells us not to trust anyone under forty. As a teenager I couldn't even comprehend the fact that I could even live to be thirty-seven. If I did, I would just be a burden on society. Where have those years gone?

The Bible asks us the question in James 4:14, *"How do you know what your life will be like tomorrow?"* and then it answers the question in the next statement. *"Your life is like the morning fog—it's here a little while, then it's gone."* Well that was encouraging! In context though, James was telling us that we have no control over the length of our life, so we need to leave it with God and, tougher yet, we need to trust Him with it. I guess Jesus summed it up when He said in Matthew 6:27, *"Can all your worries add a single moment to your life?"*

I Saw it in a Movie

"A LONG TIME AGO in a galaxy far, far away ..." So began the classic tale of good versus evil. Have you caught the re-release of *Star Wars* this month? It's hard to believe that it was twenty years ago that Luke Skywalker and his friends first came to life. What were you doing in January of 1977? I was in grade eleven and saw *Star Wars* four times that winter. The effects are a little flashier this time and, through computer wizardry, George Lucas has inserted some even stranger creatures than we saw the first time. But the story remains the same. The question is still which side of the "force" are you on?

The battle between good and evil isn't limited to the silver screen, it happens every day here in Halifax and the choice is yours. Will you serve the dark side or will you serve God? There won't be a sequel but I'll give you a hint, I've read the back of the book and we win.

HAVE YOU BEEN TO see *Titanic* yet? That has to be the premier question being asked this month. Every where you look it's *Titanic* this or *Titanic* that. The Maritime Museum of the Atlantic has a great display on the Titanic and there are several great books out there on the tragedy. It would seem that the Titanic has become the flavour of the month, that is if it really was the Titanic, but don't get me started or it'll turn into an Olympic-sized story.

The historians tell us that one of the reasons the loss of life was so great was that there weren't enough lifeboats for all the passengers. Nobody can agree if they were removed because of aesthetics or to save money, but the fact was that they had been removed.

If an analogy can be drawn between our city and the liner, then the churches of Halifax are its lifeboats and there aren't enough, for whatever reason. When we launched BCC the question that was asked over and over again was "aren't there already enough churches in Halifax?" The answer was and still is no. One of our dreams is to plant a sister church. Until we do we need to rejoice with every Faith Community Church, every Living Hope Community Church, and every Celebration Church that opens it's doors.

I Saw it in a Movie

WHO'D HAVE THUNK IT? A year ago they were calling it another *Waterworld*, and it wasn't.

They predicted it would lose more money than any other movie in history, and it didn't.

They said nobody would sit through 195 minutes of a ship sinking, but they did.

But somehow Cameron's folly didn't do what everyone thought it would, and it did what nobody expected it to do … it succeeded. They are saying now that they knew from the beginning that *Titanic* would be the greatest picture ever. Certainly the sweep at the Academy Awards proved at least the last prediction true. It's amazing how a little success can change so many people's opinion of you.

But God's love isn't conditional on our success. After all, listen to what the Bible says in the book of Romans 5:8 (CEV), *"But God showed how much he loved us by having Christ die for us, even though we were sinful."*

And that is better than a boatload of Oscars!

ANGELA AND I CAUGHT a movie a couple of weeks ago that made me stop and ponder.

It was Robin Williams' new movie *What Dreams May Come*, kind of a new-age, hodge-podge view of the hereafter. After Williams' character, a pediatrician, and his two teenage children are all killed in two separate car accidents, the story really comes to life ... so to speak. His wife, unable to cope with her grief, commits suicide and winds up in hell, eternally separated from the rest of her family who are idyllically spending their eternity in heaven.

Faced with the prospect of being separated forever from his soulmate (because, we are told, all suicides go to hell) the good doctor seeks to rescue her from her less-than-ideal circumstances.

As people left the theatre, the consensus seemed to be that all that was needed for you to get to heaven was to be a good person like Williams, who was kind, gentle, and of course funny. The movie left us with no doubt that hell was populated by suicides and lawyers.

The thought that immediately came to me as we watched the credits roll by was Proverbs 14:12: *"There is a path before each person that seems right, but it ends in death."* The good news is that the price has already been paid, and we can be rescued from hell, but the choice is yours and you have to want to be rescued.

Stupid is Forever

MONDAY THROUGH FRIDAY MY computer performs a critical function for me. Every four hours it connects itself to my phone line and calls a news provider that provides me with the very latest in Canadian and international news. Just recently it has started providing me with health news as well, and last week I received this very important warning:

"LONDON (UPI) - Some golf courses warn players not to lick their golf balls to clean them before taking a shot—they may be poisoning themselves with Agent Orange." Lick their golf balls? I guess it just goes to prove Billy Sunday's point, "Sin can be forgiven, but stupid is forever!" Lick their golf balls?

Now licking your golf balls is dumb, right? Now we know that, medically, it can affect your liver. But, consider the fact that there are people who know and believe that the only way they can get to heaven is by accepting Jesus Christ as Lord and Saviour, and they still haven't done it. You gotta wonder whether or not they lick their golf balls to clean them as well.

SOME NEWS STORIES LITERALLY cry out for a Penn of Denn to be written about them. Last winter two young women took a wrong turn on the way to a friend's house and became lost on a back road in rural Ontario. Eventually their car became stuck in the snow and caught on fire while they were trying to free it. During the twelve hours the women spent in the woods they fell through ice into a brook and walked barefoot through the snow before being rescued by a hunter.

The end result of this tragedy was that both women lost body parts to frostbite. The women and their families are now suing the Duro-Dummer Township and the property owner for not providing enough warning of the dangers of the roads. Even though they ventured onto obviously seasonal roads which were posted with "Keep Out" and "No Trespassing" signs, they feel that someone else is to blame for their tragedy.

I wonder how many people who are spiritually lost will try to place the blame on the church? Our responsibility is to reach the lost with the claims of Christ, but the lost also have a responsibility—to respond to those claims.

I'M SURE IT SEEMED like a good idea at the time. I wonder at what point he began to regret his actions. We will probably never know. Two weeks ago, the remains of twenty-seven-year-old Calvin Watson were found in the chimney of an historic building in Natchez, Mississippi. Watson had been missing since 1985. Nobody knew where he had gone and, even now, there is only speculation about what he was doing in the chimney. Fifteen years ago, the chimney led to a gift shop housed in the building. The authorities have made this statement, "His criminal record shows he was a burglar, so the suspicion is that he was crawling down the chimney to burglarize the business at that period of time, became lodged and died," Not a pretty thought at all.

Calvin Watson discovered the truth that the Bible teaches: the wages of sin is death. You're probably not planning on climbing down a chimney in the near future but even if sin does not cause your physical death, it will surely cause your spiritual death. That is unless you quit before payday and accept the gift that only God can give, eternal life.

I Read it in the News

WHAT'S WITH ALL THE mass suicides lately? It seems that every time you turn on the television or open a paper, there's been another group who have "done themselves in." The premise being, of course, that they are following a spiritual path to heaven. Obviously it must be easier to die for their beliefs than to live for them. In the latest incident, thirty-nine members of a group called "Heaven's Gate" followed their leader in a ritualistic suicide. They believed that it was the only way to be united with the aliens who were coming to take them home. Of course their leader, Marshall Applegate, may have had a different motive, it seems that he at least suggested to some of his followers that he was dying of cancer.

King Solomon wrote his book of proverbs 3000 years ago but the message is just as fresh today as when he wrote the words Proverbs 14:12, *"There is a path before each person that seems right, but it ends in death."*

Aren't you glad that you follow a God who not only promised you life, but promised you abundant life?

HOW DO YOU LOSE an airplane? Good question. Yet early in April it would appear that the United States Air Force did just that. The Colorado Civil Air Patrol is still looking for Air Force Captain Craig Button and his runaway plane.

The mystery of why Button left the Arizona-bound flight path of his three-plane team has raised speculation that he might have purposely broken away, taking his $8.8 million plane loaded with four 500-pound bombs with him. Silly me! I would have thought that there would be a little more control over something like that.

How do you lose an airplane? By not paying attention and assuming everything was all right.

How do you lose your soul? Good question. Yet this week it would appear that people all across Metro are doing just that. A plane can be replaced, a soul is gone forever. How do you lose a soul? By not paying attention and assuming that everything is all right. Let's not be responsible for souls in our care being lost.

I Read it in the News

WELL WHO'D HAVE THUNK it? Garry Kasparov got whooped by Deep Blue. "They" (whoever they are) said it would never happen; a computer would never be able to beat a human chess master. Not only did Deep Blue whoop him, but it whupped him good! In just nineteen moves IBM's super computer became the world champion chess player. Now to be fair, Kasparov had beaten the computer in the past, but IBM's whiz kids tweaked their creation since the last match and it did what "they" said could never be done.

So if'n Deep Blue can beat Kasparov … what's next? What separates man from machine? Well, when Kasparov beat Deep Blue on previous occasions, the computer didn't stalk off and claim that its opponent hadn't played fair. But maybe it would have if it had legs … who knows?

The big thing of course is that while computers were created by man, man was created by God. More importantly, we were created in God's image. Even though Deep Blue may be smarter then most of us, we can still pull its plug.

THE TWO FRONT PAGE stories this past week were worlds apart. First, Swissair Flight 111 crashed into the ocean off Peggy's Cove, and then Mark McGwire broke the single-season home run record of sixty-one set by Roger Maris in 1961.

Nothing could be further apart: an airline accident with an appalling loss of life and a sports hero paid an appalling amount of money to play a game. Yet the two events bring home the reality that we have become a society of spectators.

We watched as the tragedy of flight 111 unfolded from the futile rescue attempts to the sorrowful scenes of families trying to reconcile the beauty of Peggy's Cove with the horror of their loss. People all over North America tuned in to watch the latest events off the Nova Scotia coast.

We watched as Mark McGwire drove his sixty second home run out of the park (so to speak). The excitement was almost tangible, even through the medium of television. The day after the record had been broken, the Baseball Hall of Fame said they received over a hundred calls from people who wanted to see the bat and ball used by McGwire.

But is that all there is to life, watching? I hope not. Jesus told the apostles in John 10:10, *My purpose is to give them a rich and satisfying life.* Let's not be content to simply watch life as it goes by, but to be a part of it.

I Read it in the News

WELL, IT LOOKS LIKE the courts are going to take another look at the Clayton Johnson story. You've probably read about it in the paper, and may even remember it from the first time it was out. The gist of the story of course is that in 1993 Johnson, a Shelburne area school teacher, was tried for murder after the body of his wife was found at the foot of the basement stairs in the family home.

The evidence must have been convincing because at the time he was sentenced to prison. All during the trial and afterward, Johnson maintained his innocence, which of course is no surprise. Think of how little prison space we would need to house those who admitted to their guilt. Now, five years down the road, it appears that new forensic evidence may indicate that Mrs. Johnson died as the result of an accident.

Something that you might not know, though, is that at the time of the trial Johnson was attending a Wesleyan Church. The pastor was criticized by some people in the church because of the support he gave his parishioner. After all, everyone in the community knew the man was guilty. Well the end of that chapter was that Johnson was found guilty and went to prison, and the pastor left that church and moved on to another church.

Now if his lawyers are to be believed, their client will be vindicated. If that is the case then perhaps their client's pastor will be vindicated as well. My question is this: Even if Johnson had been guilty of murder, did his pastor do anything that he needs to be vindicated of, or was he simply doing what Jesus would do?

I'M CONFUSED AGAIN. THIS time it has to do with the murder of Matthew Shepherd, the student in Wyoming who was beaten and crucified and left to die. What confuses me is that the incident is being referred to as a hate crime. Not because of the brutality or senselessness of the act, and not because Shepherd was left hanging on a fence for almost twenty hours before being found. It isn't even being called a hate crime because Shepherd never regained consciousness before dying. The one determining factor for this vicious act of violence being denounced as a hate crime is the fact that Matthew Shepherd was openly gay.

Regardless of your stand concerning homosexuality (I'm opposed and so is the Bible), no rational human being could view Shepherd's murder as anything less than a tragedy. But surely the atrocities that he suffered could and should be defined as a crime of hatred regardless whether he was a homosexual, a heterosexual, or celibate.

Matthew Shepherd died as a result of sin, but it wasn't his sin—it was the sin of those who killed him. In most cases when one human being kills another human being it's because of hatred. That goes right back to the first murder, when Cain hated Abel and killed him. Two thousand years ago, another young man was beaten, crucified, and left to die hanging on a cross. Even though Jesus wasn't gay, the act was still an act of hatred. I'm in favour of stopping hatred directed toward homosexuals or directed toward anyone, but the solution to stopping hatred won't be found in new legislation. It will only be found through a new birth.

I Read it in the News

Defining moments. Do you ever think about the defining moments in your life? You know, the big things that make you stop and think about life. A couple of the defining moments for our generation, celebrated (if you can use that word) major anniversaries this past week. The assassination of John F. Kennedy happened thirty-five years ago this past Sunday. For many people inside and outside of the U.S. this was definitely a defining moment in their life. They can tell you where they were and what they were doing when it happened.

For example, I was three and I was playing with my building blocks on the living room floor of our home in Oromocto when the news came in. I remember thinking, "This can't be happening." Just kidding. I have no memory of that event whatsoever. On the other hand, I do remember where I was and what I was doing on November 18th, 1978, and I remember how I felt when I heard the news about the Jonestown tragedy. At eighteen years old, I couldn't comprehend what would compel 913 people to commit suicide. At thirty-eight I'm none the wiser, at least in regard to that incident.

So here's the question. Are we as committed to giving Jesus Christ our lives to live as they were in giving Jim Jones their lives to die?

Wow! It's been ten years. Who would have thought? Sometimes it seems like only yesterday it was there, and other times it seems like it's been gone forever. For the first two-thirds of my life, it was almost a constant. You read about it in the paper, you saw it on the news. Movies were made about it and the central theme of any number of novels revolved around it. One day it was there and the next day it was gone. If my kids know anything about it, they learned it in history class because it certainly isn't a current event. But this week it was, if only because it was the tenth anniversary of its demise.

I'm speaking, of course, of the Berlin wall. It was probably the greatest visual symbol of the differences between Communism and Democracy.

A much greater wall was torn down 2,000 years ago, the wall between man and God. A barrier was removed when Jesus Christ offered Himself as a sacrifice for our sins. If you haven't made the move to cross over to God, perhaps today should be the day. After all … the wall is gone.

I Read it in the News

THIRTY-FOUR YEARS IS a long time. But to some people, it was almost yesterday. I read an account this week of how Al Rascon, an American veteran, was just awarded the Medal of Honour for an act of heroism that he performed during the Vietnam war in 1966. It was just granted because the original paperwork had been lost.

After his unit was attacked, Rascon, a medic at the time, repeatedly ran into the line of fire ... treating three men, saving two of them ... despite being wounded himself. Rascon is pretty modest about the entire episode and made this statement, "I happened to have gotten shot, happened to have gotten hit by a hand grenade," he said. "So ..." He feels that the honour should have gone to his entire unit. Al Rascon may downplay the incident, but it made an incredible impact on at least two people. Neil Haffey was one of the two men whose life was saved and he made this statement, "I have four daughters and four beautiful grandchildren. I have a wonderful wife; those are all gifts from Doc." You may never have had your life saved, but if you are a Christian then you've had your eternal life saved, and that is a gift from God.

LAST WEEK I READ about a waitress in the states who was left a $10,000.00 tip on a $9.00 bar bill. It seems that she had told her British customer that she was trying to earn enough to finish her master's degree so he gave her the money. It was in all the papers, she was ecstatic, and people wondered why it couldn't have been them. Just imagine a $10,000.00 tip. It sounded almost too good to be true.

Of course the credit card company rejected the charge, the businessman sobered up and claimed that he had been duped, and the waitress is back serving drinks. In one way, she is no worse-off than she had been before, and maybe better off because the owner of the bar said that he would try to help her out because of the entire situation. So all's well that ends well. I guess.

There are people out there who think they have had an incredible offer for the hereafter, only to discover that they've been misled, and the offer wasn't real. For them the consequences are eternal. That's why Jesus said very plainly, "I am the way the truth and the life, no one comes to the Father except through me."

I Read it in the News

WHEN PIGS FLY! HOW many times have we heard that phrase, "Oh yeah? That'll happen when pigs fly." Well I don't know what you are waiting for, but take heart. US Airways confirmed that on October 17th a fully grown pig flew on their airline from Philadelphia to Seattle, first class. It would appear that the pig's owners produced a letter from a doctor showing that the pig was a therapeutic animal, much like a seeing-eye dog. Airline staff finally relented and the pig was allowed to accompany his owner on the six-hour flight. A spokesman for US Airway stated, "We can confirm that the pig travelled, and we can confirm it will never happen again. Let me stress that it will never happen again."

When I read the story, I thought as Christians we are a lot like that flying pig, making a trip that we really aren't entitled to. He flew to Seattle because of gullible airline staff; we are going to heaven because of the sacrifice of a loving God. Of course, the trip to Seattle would appear to have been a one-off thing, while the offer is still open for those who want to go to heaven.

IT HADN'T SEEMED TO matter a great deal—after all, it had been going on for over twenty years and nobody had complained. In May of this year, twenty years of lies caught up with the people of Walkerton Ontario. Falsifying records and not following up on provincial requirements set the stage for an E. Coli outbreak that left 7 people dead and over 2,000 ill in the town of 5,000. This week Stanley Koebel, the man responsible for the Walkerton water supply, acknowledged that the disaster had been caused by his neglect and apologized for the role he played.

The thing that captivated me the most was when he commented on how he had to walk a fine line between keeping the water safe and keeping the customers happy. It seemed that chlorine levels were allowed to drop so that people wouldn't complain about the taste, even if it meant the levels were no longer effective. The same people that wanted less chlorine still condemned Koebel for doing what they wanted him to do.

People sometimes ask the church to dilute the message of the cross so that it doesn't offend people. Yet on judgment day, will they blame the church for doing what they wanted it to do?

I Read it in the News

THEY ARE FREE! AFTER more than three months behind bars in Afghanistan, the eight aid workers from "Shelter Now International" are free. How much thought did we give to the eight while they were in prison? How many prayers were said for their safety and release? If I am any indication, probably not nearly enough. The group, consisting of two Americans, two Australians, and four Germans were imprisoned for seeking to convert people to Christianity. In other words, they risked their freedom and their lives to be obedient to the word of God; you remember Matthew 28:19, the great commission, when Jesus commanded us to tell others about Him.

Each one of us is a believer because somebody somewhere felt compelled to tell us about the love and forgiveness of Jesus. It was probably someone who cared a great deal about you, a friend or a family member who cared about your eternity. So here is a question. Who is there in your circle of influence waiting for you to tell them about Jesus? Chances are that you won't go to prison or be killed for your efforts. At worst you might be embarrassed, but we are talking about someone's eternity and your obedience.

IT WOULD APPEAR THAT the war on terrorism is actually a war on terrorists who target the United States. Again terror is rearing its ugly head in Israel and the western response is to seek to mediate the dispute, something that was never considered after September 11th. It's funny how military action is the answer when the west is attacked but Canadian and American leaders warn Israel about the consequences of retaliation when innocent Jews are killed.

Terrorists are terrorists whether they are blowing up the World Trade Centre in New York City or buses in Jerusalem. They are not freedom fighters, they are terrorists. Let's not forget that the people of Israel are God's people. They may be living in disobedience to His will, but they are still His children. In less than two weeks we celebrate the birth of Jesus Christ our Lord, who was a Jew. During this Christmas season we need to remember that our spiritual heritage lies in Israel and our religious heritage lies in Judaism. God will not be mocked and I'm thinking that it might be better to be on the side of His people than to side with their enemies. When we demand an end to terror, let's make sure we mean an end to terror everywhere.

I Read it in the News

DID YOU READ ABOUT Dolly in the paper last month? That's Dolly the sheep, not Dolly the singer. It was revealed on Monday that researchers in Scotland had managed to produce an exact replica of a fully grown mammal using only its cells. That's called cloning. The mammal in question was a sheep, and Dolly was the replica.

Now the fear, of course, is that if you can create a sheep by cloning then you could create a human by cloning. But we are told not to worry by one of the scientists involved who stated "There is no clinical reason why you would do this. Why would you make another human being? We think it would be ethically unacceptable, and certainly would not want to be involved in the project."

Boy, it's reassuring to know that scientists would never do anything that was ethically unacceptable. I mean, it would never happen right? We may not be able to trust man but we can still trust God. The scientists needed God to create the original sheep. Because for all they've done, they still haven't figured out how to create something out of nothing.

Politicians and Other Strange Bedfellows

IMAGINE YOU HAD A car that would only start seventy-eight percent of the time (it may not be that far a stretch for some folks), or would only stop seventy-eight percent of the time. Imagine if your doctor was only right seventy-eight percent of the time or imagine your surgeon telling you "Seventy-eight percent of my patients survive." Imagine getting on a plane that didn't crash seventy-eight percent of the time. You know what that would mean, don't you? It means that your car doesn't start twenty-two percent of the time, wouldn't stop twenty-two percent of the time (you'd better hope that it was in front of something soft). It would mean that twenty-two percent of the time your doctor would be wrong and twenty-two percent of your surgeon's patients died. It would mean that the plane crashed twenty-two percent of the time. Would you be happy with those odds? I think not!

It wasn't that long ago though that our Prime Minister told us that we should be pleased that our government had kept Seventy-eight percent of it's promises. What were the other twenty-two percent? How about the realization that they had only lied about twenty-two percent of their promises? Isn't it great to realize the truth of the Bible in Hebrews 6:18, *"It is impossible for God to lie."* Now if only the red book said something similar.

WELL, HAVE YOU MADE up your mind yet? You've had six weeks to decide, but I'd be willing to wager that you had your mind made up long before then. As a matter of fact, I suspect that there hasn't been much done or said over the past six weeks that has had much of an impact on the decision that you had already made, but then again, maybe I'm wrong. It's happened before.

I'm talking about the election of course. You did remember the election right? I mean, how could you miss the signs, ads, and television commercials? So after listening to all the hype and all the promises, you now have to intelligently cast a ballot. A daunting task to say the least, but it must be done! Some people say that it doesn't matter, because no matter who you vote for, a politician will still get in. But, as a believer you have two obligations: the first is to vote because when you give up your right to vote, you give up your right to complain. The second obligation is to pray for your leaders, whether you voted for them or not.

HE SAID HE'D DO it and now he's done it. Nobody really thought he'd do it, and he fooled them all because he did exactly what he said he'd do. My question is, why were we all so surprised? Well, I guess based on past experience we should have been surprised—not necessarily past experience with him, but with others like him. Who did it and what did they do? The answer to the first question is Frank McKenna, of course, and to the second, he stepped down as Premier of New Brunswick ten years after he was voted in, just like he said he would.

This is not an endorsement of Mr. McKenna nor a criticism, just an observation. It is a sad state of affairs when a politician keeping his word is a major news story. Maybe Mr. McKenna understands the truth of Proverbs 12:22, *"The LORD detests lying lips, but he delights in those who tell the truth."*

Whether Frank McKenna is honest or not really doesn't matter a great deal in the eternal scheme of things, but I hope that my honesty is always taken for granted and that keeping my word is never seen as a newsworthy event, just an everyday occurrence.

HERE'S A KIND OF interesting thought, Bill Clinton can be President of the United States and be accused of sexual harassment and adultery, and there's no problem with him keeping his position, yet the thought that he may have lied is enough for people to talk impeachment. It's a strange world that we live in.

I've talked to people who tell me "It's nobody's business what goes on in the President's private life." Maybe so, but I would think that a man who is capable of betraying his wife through adultery probably shouldn't be trusted to sell used cars, let alone run the most powerful country in the world. After all, Jesus said in Luke 16:10, *"If you are faithful in little things, you will be faithful in large ones. But if you are dishonest in little things, you won't be honest with greater responsibilities."*

Now it's very doubtful that any of us will ever be President of the United States, but if you're a Christian then you're an Ambassador of Jesus Christ and that carries an even greater responsibility for moral integrity.

THE BAND WAS THERE but the senator didn't show.

Senator Andrew Thompson, who now winters in Mexico, has only been in the Senate Chambers fourteen times in the last seven years. It wouldn't be so bad if he hadn't been collecting over $74,000 a year in salary and tax free benefits. Nice work if you can find it.

This past week the senate ordered Thompson to appear for work and the Reform party even hired a Mexican band to serenade the truant senator (perhaps so he wouldn't feel homesick,) but once again Thompson was a now show.

Senator Thompson obviously figures that with a minimum amount of effort he should be able to reap the maximum reward.

Sounds like some people I've met and their view of church and God. They don't want to put much in but they expect to get lots out. Much like the good senator, they see a absolutely nothing wrong with their behaviour.

It would probably be too much of a coincidence to find out that the two times that Thompson showed up each year were Christmas and Easter.

I'm NOT SURE WHO I'm more disgusted with, Bill Clinton for his immoral behaviour, or the media for the way they have covered Bill Clinton's immoral behaviour. It probably would have been sufficient for the world to know that Clinton committed some morally reprehensible acts without knowing all the details of his dirty deeds. If the President is to shoulder the primary blame for acting irresponsibly then the print media has acted just as irresponsibly in printing the lurid details.

Now I realize that I'm a big boy and I don't have to read anything that I don't want to, but my major complaint has to do with the fact that my children read the paper. Of all the things I thought I needed to shield them from, our daily papers weren't on the list, until now.

The newspapers may defend their actions as simply providing the public with what they need to know. I would debate whether or not we needed the details but I'm a little tired of either having to hide the political cartoons from my kids or trying to explain things that they don't need to know.

As believers, I trust that we haven't gotten caught up in having to know all the details and that we haven't been enjoying cartoons that up until recently would not have appeared in anything less than smutty magazines. Perhaps it's time to reflect again on Philippians 4:8 *"Fix your thoughts on what is true, and honorable, and right, and pure, and lovely, and admirable. Think about things that are excellent and worthy of praise."*

WELL IT LOOKS LIKE he still has the right stuff. In 1957 he set a transcontinental speed record when he flew across the United States in 3 hours 20 minutes and 8.4 seconds. In 1962 he became the first man to circle the earth when he made three orbits in "Friendship 7." In 1974 he became a U.S. Senator, a position he still holds, and in 1984 and 1988 he made unsuccessful bids for presidential nomination for the Democrats (would have been a little bit different president than Bill, I would suspect).

Last week he proved that he still has the right stuff when, at the age of seventy-seven, he became the oldest man ever to go into space. Think about it. When other men are enjoying their retirement and playing horseshoes, John Glenn is flying around in the Space Shuttle Discovery. What a hoot! Is he being silly? Is he too old for stuff like that? Only Glenn can answer those questions, but what he has done has been an inspiration to seniors all over the world who are saying, "If John Glenn can go into space at his age what can I do?"

Glenn ought to be an example not just to the elderly but to every one of us who claims Christ's promise in John 10:10 "*I have come that everyone would have life, and have it in its fullest.*" You might not be able to fly around the world, but you can have an impact with your life. But only if you decide you want to.

NEWSMAKER OF THE CENTURY … that has to be some kind of honour, especially if you are around to have it bestowed upon you.

Being a Trudeau fan from way back, I was quite pleased to see the honour bestowed upon Pierre Elliot and, of course, I think he deserves it. Even those who mildly dislike our former PM (can anyone mildly dislike Trudeau?) have to admit that he made for a lot of news. The award has nothing to do with his accomplishments or positive virtues, simply the amount of press that he generated.

At eighty he can still generates press. Probably the main thing that makes Trudeau tick is his passion for Canada. Every decision that he made whether good or bad, in his mind, was made for his country.

So, I guess the question is, what is your passion? You have to have a passion, it's what adds colour to your life. Is it your faith, your family, your work? Of course just saying that it's your passion doesn't make it so. It's how you live your life, what you make your sacrifices for, and where your priorities lie. In the last month of the last year of this century, perhaps it would be a good time to establish what our passion will be for the next century.

THE QUESTION IS THIS: will we know who our new prime minister is before our neighbours know who their new president is? Well, actually, that isn't the question at all, I just made it up, but it's worth thinking about. Personally I think that at this point, Gore and Bush should have to wrestle for the job.

How you feel about the American electoral system compared to the Canadian system is irrelevant. What is relevant is that in both of our countries we have the great privilege of democracy, and like all other privileges, it is only worth something if we choose to exercise it. The tragedy in the recent US election wasn't how close it was. That's just fun. It's that almost half of the eligible voters chose not to participate in the process. In a little over a week you will have your chance to participate in the political forum. I trust that you will exercise that privilege. Remember, when you give up your privilege to vote, you give up your right to complain. Also remember that, as believers, our responsibility does not stop with voting, because in God's word we have been commanded to pray for whoever is elected on the 27th.

HOW WOULD YOU FEEL? Here you are, the most powerful and undoubtedly most protected man in the world. One minute you're munching pretzels and watching a football game, the next minute you wake up on the floor with a bruise on your cheek and your two dogs are giving you funny looks. You gotta hate that. This past week it was reported that President Bush passed out after choking on a pretzel. All I could think was, what if he had died? What a legacy! You can imagine the Trivial Pursuit question in the 2200 edition, "Which American President choked to death on a pretzel?" Once I got that mental picture out of my mind, I realized how fragile life was, even for someone as well protected as George W. Bush. Not only are the Secret Service hovering around him almost all the time (notice the use of the word almost), but his health is constantly being monitored. Yet one pretzel did what an armed assailant would have a tough time doing. A reminder that it's not enough to plan on getting things straight with God later, because there is no guarantee of a later—not even if you are the most powerful and most protected man in the world.

Things that Make You Go Hmmmmm

WELL, OUR LOT IS now grassed. It looks a lot different green than it did brown. On Friday there was nothing. By Tuesday evening it was a lawn. But, I was a little concerned about the sod we laid. You see, when I was talking to the nursery guy, he told me that the sod was demon possessed. Honest! At least I think that's what he meant when he told me that during the first week I'd have to water the hell out of it. I wanted to ask him how hell got in there in the first place but decided that discretion was the better part of valour.

I'm sure that part of Satan's strategy to ensnare people is to trivialize hell so that it's no longer taken seriously. Hell has become such a commonplace part of many people's everyday conversations that it is no longer a threat. The fact is … Hell is a reality. It's not in my grass, there's only one way to avoid it, and that's not by watering it.

Jesus said in John 14:6, *"I am the way, the truth, and the life. No one can come to the Father except through me."* Don't know if it'll do much for my grass, but I plan on it keeping me out of Hell.

THIS HOT WEATHER MUST be having a strange effect on people. Just last week, three Yemeni men sued NASA, claiming that NASA's Sojourner robot was trespassing on their planet. The planet in question is Mars. Ok. Adam Ismail, Mustafa Khalil, and Abdullah al-Umari claim that they inherited the red planet from their ancestors three thousand years ago and that NASA needed to get their permission before Sojourner made its historic landing.

Ok. What I want to know is ... did they get it in writing? If they didn't, don't they realize that a verbal contract is only as good as the paper it's written on?

As Christians we have an inheritance as well ... one that was given to us almost 2,000 years ago. Paul tells us in Colossians 3:23-24, *"Work willingly at whatever you do, as though you were working for the Lord rather than for people. Remember that the Lord will give you an inheritance as your reward, and that the Master you are serving is Christ."* The great part is ... we've got it in writing.

The question remains though ... is the inheritance yours? You're the only one who can answer that and you're the only one who can claim it.

I'M A LITTLE CONFUSED! Well, some things go without saying. This time I'm confused over a couple of recent articles in *the Chronicle* and *the Daily News*. It was the result of an interview with the new moderator of the largest Protestant denomination in Canada. My confusion arises from how the leader of a "Christian" church can deny the deity of Jesus Christ, the authority of the Bible, and the reality of the here-after? Now you know that I'm not a church-basher, but should an organization that denies the very foundation of the Christian faith call itself a "Christian" church?

If we were to enact the "Truth-in-advertising" laws, wouldn't it have to rename itself a community agency or a social club? "But Denn," you say, "That's not the view of the church, just the view of its leadership." Ahhhhh! Well that explains it.

My question is if Mr. Phipps doesn't believe that Jesus was the Son of God, doesn't believe that Jesus rose from the dead, and isn't sure that there is a heaven or hell, what does he believe?

THEY SAID THEY'D DO it, and they didn't. For a week all we heard was, "We're going to do it, just watch us." They said they'd do it. They didn't. The postal union spent the better part of a week threatening to walk off the job Wednesday at midnight and then they didn't. Go figure.

Not that it mattered a great deal to me, I use e-mail for my letters, pay my bills electronically, get my packages by courier, and phone my parents. Maybe they realized that it wasn't really a threat; after all, the only thing I seem to get by mail is bills.

But you'd think that since they said they'd do it, they would have gone ahead and done it.

A lot of people hoping that hell is going to be like that. They know that the Bible, the Word of God, says that without Jesus Christ they will go to hell, but they're hoping that God was just kidding. You know He made the threat but He really doesn't plan on carrying it out.

Maybe they need to check out 1 Samuel 15:29, *"And he who is the Glory of Israel will not lie, nor will he change his mind, for he is not human that he should change his mind!"*

I SAW A SIGN in the window of the "Body Shop" the other day. It said "Wise gifts make up for wicked ways." I thought to myself, "That's interesting theology." But when you think about it, that pretty much represents the way many people view their salvation. They are constantly in fear that the good things they do won't outweigh the mistakes that they make or the sins that they commit.

The bad news is they are right! According to the Word of God we can never do enough good things to make God happy. The good news, however, is that Jesus Christ gives us the ultimate gift in the forgiveness that He offers. During this Christmas season, when gift-giving and gift-getting is on everyone's minds … take time to focus on the gift that God gives, the greatest gift of all. Paul tells us about it in Romans 6:23, *"For the wages of sin is death, but the free gift of God is eternal life through Christ Jesus our Lord."*

The question is have you got your gift yet or are you still working for wages? The sign was right. His wise gift makes up for our wicked ways.

WHY WOULD TWO SEEMINGLY-BRIGHT and articulate teenagers lay down on a railroad track and allow themselves to be run over by an oncoming train? Why? That question is being asked by faculty and students alike at Robert Land Academy, an exclusive boarding school in Ontario.

Just last week, two of their students, a sixteen-year-old and a seventeen-year-old, ended their lives in what authorities speculated was either a bizarre suicide pact or a game of chicken that went seriously wrong. Of course there is a third scenario: they were simply sleeping on the tracks (less sinister perhaps, but really stupid).

By any account, the question still has to be asked: Why? It's a question that will probably remain unanswered. The reality is that the reason why is irrelevant. The consequences were deadly.

Why would seemingly bright and articulate people who know the consequences of not accepting Jesus as Saviour continue on in life, knowing that at their death they face the certainty of a Christ-less eternity? The reality is that the reason why is irrelevant. The consequences are deadly.

ANGELA AND I SAT in a restaurant last week and watched a small room of people absently feeding loonies into VLTs. (You can tell we only eat in the very finest of dining establishments.) As we watched, I became convinced of the truth of the remark, "VLTs are a tax on the mathematically challenged." They can join the other people who are really bad at math; you know ... the ones who buy lottery tickets.

What compels people to throw away their money? I mean really, what are their chances of winning? Yet the allure of getting lots for a little is still there.

People gamble in many different ways, even the government gambles that they are making more in the revenue then what they are paying out in the social cost. In the long run though, most of what people have to lose can be replaced, one way or another.

Perhaps the saddest cases are the people who gamble with their eternity, playing against the odds that they can live for the Devil all their lives but turn to God just before they die. I've got bad news for them. That probably isn't going to happen. Why gamble with where you will spend eternity when Jesus offers us guaranteed access to heaven?

I READ RECENTLY THAT the Russian parliament passed a bill making it specifically illegal for people to eat their pets. Now if you stop and think this one through, you'll realize that the only logical reason for this legislation must be that people were actually eating their pets.

I mean, if nobody was eating their pets, there wouldn't have to be a law preventing it, am I right? Then I wondered, "What's a pet?" Does this law mean that you wouldn't be able to eat your pet chicken? How would they differentiate between a "pet chicken" and just a plain, ordinary "eating chicken"? I'm not sure that all pets would make good eating, but I wonder if the choice was eat Fido or starve, what would our decision be?

Where am I going with this? I'm not sure, but some things are too good not to share. Wait. I have it. Have we taken the time lately to express thanks to the Father, not only have we not had to eat our pets to survive but also we haven't even had to consider it! The very concept of eating your pet is so foreign that it seems almost inconceivable, and that in itself is worthy of thanks.

I WAS READING AN article on Cross Cultural Church Planting the other day and came across a statement that read, "America has the second largest African-American population next to Nigeria." My first question was, how many African-Americans do they have in Nigeria? It's interesting how our language changes and we accept statements as correct even though they obviously aren't. Not that the term *African-American* is wrong, any more than Irish-Canadian or French-Canadian would be wrong. However, to make that term inclusive to mean anyone of African descent seems to be a little condescending.

Sometimes we need to swallow our intense desire for political correctness and use the proper term. Often at Bedford Community Church we refer to those who don't know Christ as pre-Christians. Perhaps that's why we don't feel an urgency to reach them. After all, how bad can it be just being a pre-Christian? Perhaps it's time to readjust our focus and realize that because they are pre-Christians they aren't Christians at all, and because they aren't Christians, the Bible says they are lost, and because they are lost they will spend their eternity separated from a God they never knew. Maybe knowing that will break our hearts.

I'M CONFUSED. I KNOW that's not unusual, but bear with me on this one. On Saturday there was an article in the paper about a recent Angus Reid Report that stated eighty-four percent of Canadians believed in God and sixty-seven percent felt that their religion was very important in their everyday life.

Now I'm not confused about the eighty-four percent who claimed to believe in God, they're just trying to cover all their bases. It's the sixty-seven percent who felt that religion was very important in their everyday life that confused me. Think about it, sixty-seven percent. I want to know where they are. There are over 15,000 people in the Bedford area. So, if sixty-seven percent feel that religion is very important in their lives, there should be 10,000 people in church in Bedford on Sunday mornings. There ain't. As a matter of fact there's probably fewer than 2,000 people in church in Bedford on an average Sunday morning.

My assumption would be that while their religion might be important, it's not relevant to their day-to-day life. My prayer for you is that your relationship with God will not only be important but will also be relevant and real.

Things that Make You Go Hmmmmm

THEY ARE A TRADITIONAL group, they've been meeting together for almost a hundred years and they are very passionate about their beliefs. That's where the problem lies. In recent years the group has become divided into two camps. The traditionalists are standing by their traditions, declaring that any compromise of their values will destroy the group. The other side is seen as liberals who are set to destroy what the group stands for and has always stood for. But they defend their actions by saying if standards aren't relaxed, the group will no longer attract younger members and will in all probability not be able to keep the children who are a part of the group now. Their reasoning is that the standards of the group are out of step with society and are no longer relevant to this time and culture.

The scenario sounds familiar; churches have been having this debate for years. In this case, though, it's not a church. It's a group called "The Free Body Culture," a naturalist group in Europe. The traditionalists insist the long-standing tradition of total nudity at all group functions remain, while the liberals say that people should have the choice to wear clothes at some times. And you thought the church had problems with change.

THEY SAY IT'S FUN, and I'll have to take their word for it. They say it's not to be missed, and once again I'll have to take their word for it. It's something that I've periodically thought about, but usually the urge passed as quickly as it arrived. Now, well, now I have an excuse. You see I read today in the paper that middle-aged, sedentary males shouldn't take part in the annual polar bear dips. After my initial disappointment faded, I read the rest of the article and discovered that at least one cardiologist was warning of the possible dangers associated with plunging one's body into subzero water on the first day of the year. Like that's a no brainer. The interesting thing was the response from a number of the Polar Bear Clubs, who maintained that their members would continue to make the annual dip with or without the endorsements of the medical establishment.

That's just like life. When there's something we want to do, we do it. It doesn't matter how many people warn us about the possible consequences. The physical consequences can often be serious, but when we don't heed spiritual warnings, the consequences can be eternal.

It Looked Like …

NEW JERSEY? I MEAN, face it. If you were the Virgin Mary and you had to choose a spot to appear to the world, would it be a supermarket freezer door in Jersey City? According to the media it happened, and the media wouldn't try to deceive us, would they?

According to witnesses, the image, appearing between the windows of a freezer full of burritos and sausages, was said to be the silhouette of a woman in a hooded garment. The apparition first appeared on Thursday and lasted through the weekend. During that time hundreds of visitors left candles, flowers, and handwritten notes at the foot of the freezer.

New Jersey? The location being put aside for the moment, we hear of these visitations from time to time, including on a tree in our own city last year, but what I want to know is why? Why would Mary leave heaven to appear in Jersey City or for that matter Halifax?

Is it much different in the Evangelical church? Super stars and strange happenings can still draw bigger crowds than praising God and hearing the Word of God preached can. Without discounting what has happened in some churches, some of it's not a whole lot less strange than the Virgin's appearance last week. I guess Jesus was right when he said in John 4:48, *"You won't have faith unless you see miracles and wonders!"*

I WANT TO START by saying that I like a cup of coffee as much as the next guy—maybe even more than the next guy, depending on who the next guy is. Let it be noted that the first thing I wanted after landing back in the Maritimes from Australia was a Tim Horton's coffee and donut. But I'm confused. Why would people flock to the Bras D'Or Tim Horton's in Cape Breton to see a Christ-like image that had appeared on the outside wall last week? Presumably some people who wouldn't go to church to meet Him personally would make the trip to a Timmy's to see his face. The image didn't do anything, people didn't credit it with healing them or saving their marriage, but they still came out in droves to see it. I wonder what the last thing was in Bras D'or to cause a traffic jam?

All of the questions are pointless because after management changed the outside light bulbs Jesus disappeared. Oh well. Aren't you glad that the Jesus you serve isn't dependent on which light bulb you're using? For that matter, it's great to know that your relationship with Jesus isn't dependent on how you feel, or what type of day you're having, or anything else. Jesus said in John 14:18-19, *"No, I will not abandon you as orphans—I will come to you. Soon the world will no longer see me, but you will see me. Since I live, you also will live."* But even without the face on the wall, we all know that there's always time for Tim Horton's.

It Looked Like ...

WE MUST BE A great province; it seems like every year the Virgin Mary shows up in one of our smaller communities, so we must be doing something right. Last year she was on a tree in Halifax, the year before she appeared at a Tim Horton's in Cape Breton, and just recently she's been sighted on a freshly painted bedroom wall in Indian Brook. People who very seldom seek God in church or in the Bible have made their way to Tina Sack's small home looking for miracles ranging from healings to good luck on the lottery.

I have no opinion on what the image in the blue paint actually is—well I do have an opinion, but I'm not going to tell you what it is.

I just marvel that people who have no time for God are lining up to see the Virgin Mary on a bedroom wall. It's also interesting to notice that very little attention is given to Jesus, even though He is supposedly a part of the image. Folks, you don't have to drive to Indian Brook. God has told us in His word, if you look for me wholeheartedly, you will find me.

You Gotta Hate That!

IT WAS A TRAGEDY, a senseless tragedy. Eight lives were destroyed and countless others were shattered. When the minivan carrying ten pre-schoolers crossed into the oncoming lane outside of St-Jean-Baptiste-Nicolet last week, it changed the lives of the village of 2,800 forever. The two drivers involved will live with their memories and their doubts until they die. God will be blamed! I can already hear the comments, "How could God allow such a thing?" or "Where was God when the accident happened?" Of course we all know that God wasn't to blame for what happened last week. It wasn't God who put too many children in the van, it wasn't God who strapped three kids to a belt, and it wasn't God who swerved into oncoming traffic. Yes, God could have prevented it, and so could the driver of the van.

I have mentioned before the greatest gift that God ever gave us was our free will, the ability to make choices for ourselves. But it's a double-edged sword, we can't accept the gift of being allowed to do as we wish and still have God bail us out of our mistakes. What happened last week was a tragedy, a senseless tragedy, but it wasn't God's fault.

THEY THOUGHT THEY WERE safe. Deep in their hearts they knew that they had done the right thing, that most of the danger had passed, and they were safe. And then the small safe world that was theirs was suddenly destroyed, and them along with it.

I spent a couple of years at sea in my teens, and my family has gone to sea for several generations. When there are stories of shipwrecks in the paper, I read them with the understanding. "There but for the grace of God …" So this past week when the Greek carrier "Leader L." went down, my horror multiplied when I read about the dozen men who were lost after they had made their way to safety in an enclosed lifeboat. The problem was that their lifeboat was still tied to the ship when it sank. I could only imagine what went through their minds when their safe haven turned into a communal coffin. My first thought was, how many people are there who think they are safe for eternity, but who have tied their salvation to the wrong thing?

You Gotta Hate That!

IT WAS JUST GOING to be a night of partying, just a little fun with the other teens, but it turned into a tragedy that thrust the tiny community of Hare Bay, Newfoundland, into the national spotlight. We've all shaken our heads in dismay over the news, students in this small town mistakenly thought the green liquid in the pop bottle was "Screech" or "Moonshine" when in reality it was antifreeze. As a result, two of the teens died of methanol poisoning and two others remain in the hospital in serious condition.

But it wasn't supposed to be that way. Other teens who were at the party tell about those who drank the liquid having a good time, laughing and carrying on. It was only the next day that the consequences of their actions began to happen. The severe symptoms that accompany methanol poisoning only start to appear ten-to-eighteen hours after it is consumed. As I read the stories, I realized that it's like any sin in our lives, very seldom does it have immediate consequences. That is why the Bible talks about the "fleeting pleasures of sin." It doesn't deny there is pleasure, but it is only fleeting. God's gift, our salvation, lasts forever.

HALF-NAKED AND BLEEDING, they had been beaten and left for dead. All that was needed was for somebody, anybody, to stop and help. It should have been easy—their attacker was long gone—but nobody stopped and nobody called for help. As sad as the story is, it's not indicative of our culture or our times but of human nature.

It is as fresh as last week's news, but it didn't happen last week. It happened 2,000 years ago. And it didn't happen in Montreal, it happened between Jerusalem and Jericho. Jesus told the story of the Good Samaritan to illustrate our need to love our neighbours, but people apparently still haven't caught on. The story of the Good Samaritan was played out last week in front of a Montreal Call Centre, when a teenage girl was left unconscious on a sidewalk for three hours before anyone called for help. But exhibiting love for our neighbours doesn't have to wait for the spectacular, we need to daily live our love, exhibiting it in how we treat everyone we come in contact with. If we help others with little things, then it will be second nature to respond with love in a crisis.

HAVE YOU EVER FOUND yourself going the wrong way on a one-way street? It's kind of disconcerting. You don't know what to do: stop, turn, or just keep going. Think how the captain of the *Asia Lion* felt this past week. Navigating the English Channel without the proper charts, Captain Zheng narrowly avoided two head-on collisions after he mistakenly guided his tanker, loaded with 30,000 ton of aviation fuel, the wrong way up a one-way shipping lane in the world's busiest waterway. You have to wonder, what was he thinking? The ship's owners said that it was Zheng's first trip through the Channel and that he was confused. I guess! My question is why didn't he have any charts? What made him think he could make the trip without them?

But then again, how often have we tried to navigate through our Christian life without referring to the charts? God has provided us with the directions we need in His Word, the Bible. When we find ourselves going the wrong way, most times it could have been averted if we had only looked in the book. The reason we have it is so we can read it. If we don't read it, it's nobody's fault but our own.

What's on the Tube?

WHO THINKS THESE THINGS up? I always thought people watched TV to escape reality, but the phenomenon dubbed reality TV seems to be here for another season at least. Survivor is the one everyone is talking about, but it's only one of a number of voyeur television shows set to air over the next several weeks. The one causing the biggest stir is *Temptation Island.* The new hour-long reality series is about four young couples that are shipped off to a lush resort on an island off Belize, and then tempted to stray from their relationships by a series of swinging singles.

Probably should have called it "The Devil's Playground." It's interesting to note that one of the original couples was dismissed from the show after five episodes had been filmed because it was discovered that they had a child. So the lesson we learn is it's all right for childless people to cheat in a relationship but not for parents. It would appear that the producers of the show didn't want to be responsible for destroying a relationship where there was a child involved. Now if only the producers of children would take the same view.

I SAW A TELEVISION commercial the other day that really bugged me, which is unusual, because normally I find commercials fun. But not this one, this one set my teeth on edge. It was an advertisement for CBC's children's programming and that didn't bug me. They started off showing Mister Dress-Up and that didn't bug me, and then they panned to Sesame Street, and that didn't bug me either. What bugged me was when they made the statement "We are here to teach your children right from wrong, right from left." Well, I have no problem with them teaching my kids right from left, but having a television network say they are going to teach my children right from wrong ... it would be like government teaching them financial responsibility or Bill Clinton teaching them ethics.

Did I happen to mention how much this particular commercial bugged me? The scary thing is that a lot of people have been taught right from wrong through television, and you wonder why we live in such a messed up society.

The Bible says, "You know what is right because you have been taught His law." If you're looking for His law, it's found in the Bible not on CBC!

What's on the Tube?

Aboat Time

WELL THE WEATHER OUTSIDE is frightful … Actually it's not all that bad out, but when it gets too cold to be out on the boat, the weather outside is frightful. Fall is upon us and Old Man Winter can't be far behind, which means that for the next six months boating will be but a fond memory. So, what is there to do until she's back in the water? Glad you asked. Here are some suggestions to while away those cold, boatless days of winter.

Grab a book and read about the sea. Buy the latest Clive Cussler novel. You know, the one where ocean adventurer Dirk Pitt and his latest beautiful girlfriend struggle against the forces of evil, aided only by the vast resources of the National Underwater and Marine Agency. Actually, that could be any Clive Cussler novel, so take your pick. If Dirk and his fancy gadgets don't interest you then try a classic. A few hours reading about the exploits of Horatio Hornblower or wading through *Two Years Before the Mast* should help quench your thirst for the sea.

Not into reading? Then pop some corn, snuggle down in front of the tube and watch a video. Two hours of *Dead Calm* or the *The Perfect Storm* should assure you that the best place for you and your boat is on dry ground. With that said, make sure you watch them now, not in the spring. In the spring *Twister* or *Dante's Peak* would be good choices to lead you back to the sea.

Take some time and sort through your bills from last season's repairs on the old girl. This will help remind you of why you don't boat twelve months out of the year: you can't afford to. Just don't let your wife catch you or she'll remind you of all the nice things you could have if it wasn't for "That Thing." I'm sure a university education for the children isn't all it's cracked up to be.

Give serious consideration to your wife's suggestion to turn your boat into a planter. I don't think so!

Listen to all of your Great Big Sea CDs. Sit back, relax

and pop in the Boys from the Rock. As you close your eyes and listen to *Lukey's Boat, Great Big Sea* and *Excursion Around the Bay:* you'll almost be able to feel the deck move beneath your feet and smell the salt in the air. Or maybe that's just me.

Make out a Christmas list of all the boat stuff you need for next year and remind Santa what a good person you've been. There's always room for a little creative fiction here.

And my favourite "waiting for boating weather to return activity:" mope around the house and continually remind people how many days are left before you can get the boat back in the water. Not only will this give you something to do, it'll drive the rest of the family nuts.

Until next time, remember ... the pointy end is the bow.

I WANDERED BY THE squadron the other day, just to make sure the boat was still there. It was. As I looked out over the forest of bare masts and flapping tarps I thought, "There's nothing more depressing then a boat yard in the winter, except maybe a ski hill in the summer." Then again, I don't ski, so I guess there's nothing more depressing then a boat yard in the winter.

If the downside of winter is no boating, then the upside of winter is the boat show. You know what the boat show means? That's right, boats. Even more importantly, boat stuff. All kinds of bright shiny boat stuff. Stuff that I don't need yet, but only because I haven't seen it yet.

This year I have some suggestions for boat stuff I'd like to see at the show:

1) The Cloak of Invisibility. If you are like me, you can slide your craft alongside anything, anytime, anywhere without a hitch. Show me a wharf and I will perform flawless docking maneuvers. Unless, of course, someone is watching. Same boat, same wharf, but put two or three people just standing there watching me and Mr. Murphy becomes the Captain: Everything that can go wrong will go wrong. I bump, I bang, and I end up looking like a complete fool. But with the Cloak of Invisibility, that will all be in the past. If there are people on the wharf, you just push the button and presto—captain, crew, and vessel will all be rendered invisible. It doesn't matter how bad the docking goes, the spectators will only wonder about the bump they felt.

2) The "I told you so" Eliminator. This handy dandy device really comes into its own when I mess up. That means it will probably be the most used device on board. Whenever things go wrong with docking, mooring, navigation, maintenance, or whatever, and the crew gets ready to remind you of their previous advice, you will just point the Eliminator. It's like magic. Instead of uttering the dreaded, "I told you so," they speak

terms of encouragement like, "Way to go skipper" and "I wish I had thought of that."

3) The Practically Perfect Paint. This one innovation will single-handedly reduce your workload by half because everyone will be happy with the colour paint you put on the boat. No more will you hear, "Have you ever thought of a deeper shade of blue?" or "Red would be pretty." Instead everyone who looks at your boat will see it in the colour of their choice regardless of how bizarre the colour actually is. (Don't ask me about the "Yellow Year.") Of course, another option would simply be a paint that looked the same on my trim as it looked on their paint chart. But that would be a little too easy, wouldn't it?

So those are some of my suggestions for Boat Stuff that I'd like to see this year.

Hope you have a great time at the boat show. Remember, the pointy end is the bow.

Aboat Time

IT'S SPRING-TIME, IT'S spring-time. The sun is shining, the birds are singing, and it's time to get the boat ready for the summer. With that in mind, I recall with fondness the words of my father. He would often look my way and say, "Spring has sprung, the grass has riz, I wonder where the birdies is?" This of course has nothing at all to do with boating. What he said about boating was; "Get off your lazy butt and get to work scraping that hull."

You see, if the good news about spring is that summer and boating are just around the corner, the bad news about spring is that before you can go boating you have to get the boat ready to go boating.

So it was in those early days when we had bought our first boat that I discovered the three basic truths of boating life (at least the three basic truths of boating life that have to do with spring): 1) It will take longer than you expect. 2) It will cost more then you figured it would. 3) You will have absolutely no friends from May until July.

Now, the first two weren't really discoveries. They are just facts of life. It doesn't matter if it's your boat you're working on or your house or your car, you inevitably overestimate your ability and underestimate the final cost. As the Canadian navy has recently discovered, all of the above rules apply to used submarines as well.

The friend thing, on the other hand, was confusing. I mean, I have friends. At least l think I have friends. Why, it was just last summer that we had people on the boat. They ate our food, they drank our drinks, and they enjoyed our company. At least they said they enjoyed our company. Maybe they just enjoyed our boat. That wasn't just an isolated case, it happened all summer. As long as the boat was in the water, we had more friends then we knew what to do with. At one point I thought we were going to have to make up a schedule so all of our friends would get a chance to go boating.

But that was last summer and the boat was in the water.

Now it's spring, the boat is in the yard, and I haven't seen any of my friends for weeks now. It's gotten to the point that if I want to talk to anyone I have to use a pay phone so Caller ID doesn't give me away. I'm beginning to feel like the Little Red Hen.

So I have decided that this year I'm tearing out four of the bunks, tossing all but two of the deck chairs over the side, and getting rid of all the extra dishes and cutlery. After all, I don't want to be lying when I say; "Gee, I don't think we'll have room for anyone else this weekend."

Until next time, remember, the bow is the pointy end!

Summer is finally here. With summer comes good weather, and good weather is boating weather, which is good because after the winter I am ready to go boating. That probably explains why I love summer. However, every year before I actually take the boat out for the first time, I go to my secret place, take out my rules for boating, and study them to make sure that I'm ready for another year. This year you are in luck because for the first time ever these rules are available to everyone.

1) Right is starboard and left is port. Through the years people have come up with various ways to remember rule number one, such as port and left both have four letters. I have discovered that they can be easily remembered by keeping in mind right is starboard and left is port.

2) The bow is the pointy end. This doesn't necessarily hold true for canoes and Boston-Whalers.

Learning the first two rules is very important because some people apparently don't know how to say right and left, front and back. Instead they say silly things like, "There's a vessel approaching off the starboard bow." At that point, if you are familiar with rule number one and two, you will know there is another boat ahead of you to the right.

3) Don't run into anything. This is very important, and anything can be better defined as anything. This includes docks, other boats, rocks, other boats, water skiers … did I mention other boats? If you fail to observe rule number three you will need to learn rules four and five.

4) When they say, "We'll have her back in the water by Tuesday," it means absolutely nothing.

5) When they say, "That shouldn't cost too much to fix," see rule number four.

6) Water inside your vessel is very seldom a good sign (unless it came aboard in a container and has remained in the container). Water inside you vessel may indicate that you did

not pay attention to rule number three.

7) When you buy your first boat you start with a bag full of luck and an empty bag of experience. The trick is to fill the bag of experience before you empty the bag of luck. I have discovered that the experience bag will be partly emptied over the winter but the converse doesn't always hold true of the luck bag. You ever notice that people never associate experience with good things? When was the last time anyone ever asked you, "Have you had any experience with having a BBQ on a beautiful day on the lake?" Never? But people do ask, "Have you ever had any experience with your BBQ exploding and blowing a hole in your boat?"

8) Remember that it's usually better to be on shore wishing you were out on your boat than to be on your boat wishing you were on shore. The first is inspired by boredom, the second is usually inspired by panic.

Until next time, remember, the pointy end is the bow.

"SHE'S" NOT A "SHE" anymore. For as long as "she's" been a part of my life "she's" been a "she." I always referred to her as "her." But no longer. I guess the time has come for me to change my errant ways and step up to the plate of political correctness. The prestigious Lloyd's List, the 268 year old publication, that claims to be the oldest daily newspaper, has recently announced that they will no longer refer to ships using the feminine pronoun. In explanation, Julian Bray, the editor, wrote: "The shipping industry does need to move forward if it is not to risk becoming a backwater of international business. I decided that it was time to catch up with the rest of the world, and most other news organizations refer to ships as neuter."

Now, I will admit that referring to a vessel named the John F. Kennedy as a "she" seems a little strange, although it might have made a little more sense with a ship named the J. Edger Hoover!

As far as I know, when Noah finally had finished building the Ark, he stood back and said "Well, there 'she' is." But the question lingers, why? Why have boats of all shapes and sizes been referred to as female entities since the beginning of time? A spokesman for the Royal Navy stated; "Ships have a soul. If I remember my history, they are female because originally the ship was the only woman allowed at sea and was treated with deference and respect—and because they are expensive." Others feel that the use of the feminine pronoun has it's origins with the wives of seafarers who saw boats as the other women, so you would get comments like "I suppose you'll be spending the weekend with 'her' again!"

Personally, I've always referred to my cars and boats as "she" because I could never figure out all their mysteries but they sure were lots of fun to be around. However, not being satisfied to simply wonder why boats were girls and wanting to find a more profound reason for the tradition; I conducted a highly scientific survey. That is, I asked a half-a-dozen of the guys that I hang around with why boats were called "she." The final analysis was because they are "she's." You refer to your mother as she, your wife as she, and your daughter as "she," so why wouldn't you refer to your boat as "she?" Besides, if we don't call our boat "she," what will we call her? "It" sounds too much like how you'd refer to your neutered German shepherd.

I wandered down to the squadron the other day and, after looking the old girl all over, I decided that there wasn't much chance of her ending up in Lloyd's List, unless Uncle Lloyd was planning on coming aboard this weekend. So I think I'll go along with the chap from the Royal Navy who said "Lloyd's List can do what it wants. The Royal Navy will continue to call its ships 'she' as we always have done."

Until next time, remember, the pointy end is the bow.